Remembering Christmas

**Compiled and Edited
by Yvonne Lehman**

Broken Arrow, OK

Scripture quotations marked ESV are taken from *The Holy Bible, English Standard Version*. ESV® Permanent Text Edition® (2016). Copyright © 2001 by Crossway Bibles, a publishing ministry of Good News Publishers. Used by pemission.

Scripture quotations marked NASB are taken from the *New American Standard Bible* Copyright © 1960, 1962, 1963, 1968, 1971, 1972, 1973, 1975, 1977, 1995 by The Lockman Foundation. Used by permission.

Scripture quotations marked NKJV are taken from the *New King James Version*®. Copyright © 1982 by Thomas Nelson. Used by permission. All rights reserved.

Scripture quotations marked NIV are taken from the *The Holy Bible, New International Version*. Copyright © 1973, 1978, 1984, International Bible Society. Used by permission of Zondervan. All rights reserved.

Royalties for this book are donated to Samaritan's Purse.

REMEMBERING CHRISTMAS
ISBN-13: 978-1-60495-059-5

Copyright © 2019 by Yvonne Lehman. Published in the USA by Grace Publishing. All rights reserved. No part of this book may be reproduced in any form or by any electronic or mechanical means, including information storage and retrieval systems, without permission in writing, except as provided by USA Copyright law.

From Samaritan's Purse

We so appreciate your donating all royalties to Samaritan's Purse from the sale of the books *Divine Moments, Christmas Moments, Spoken Moments, Precious Precocious Moments, More Christmas Moments, Stupid Moments, Additional Christmas Moments, Loving Moments, Merry Christmas Moments, Cool-inary Moments, Moments with Billy Graham, Personal Titanic Moments,* and now *Remembering Christmas* to Samaritan's Purse.

What a blessing that you would think of us! Thank you for your willingness to bless others and bring glory to God through your literary talents. Grace and peace to you.

Their Mission Statement:

Samaritan's Purse is a nondenominational evangelical Christian organization providing spiritual and physical aid to hurting people around the world.

Since 1970, Samaritan's Purse has helped victims of war, poverty, natural disasters, disease, and famine with the purpose of sharing God's love through his son, Jesus Christ.

Go and do likewise
Luke 10:37

You can learn more by visiting their website at
www.samaritanspurse.org

Contents

Remembering... – Yvonne Lehman 7
1. *The Same Story as Last Year* – Gina Stinson 8
2. *A Perfect Christmas* – Lana Newton 10
3. *Here Comes Santa Claus* – Phil Gladden 14
4. *A Heart Full of Questions* – Kathleen Kohler 16
5. *Wrapped in Humanity* – Norma C. Mezoe 20
6. *He's Always Watching* – Lynn Watson 21
7. *A First Christmas Present* – Shirley Alday 23
8. *Christmas Memories* – Lorilyn Roberts 25
9. *Christmas Tradition* – Lisa Braxton 28
10. *The Gift* – Helen L. Hoover 31
11. *The Crocheted Angel* – Sherry Diane Kitts 34
12. *Operation Pony* – Candy Arrington 37
13. *The Falling Tree* – Melissa Henderson 39
14. *Noel Reflections* – Lydia E. Harris 42
15. *Just One More Child* – Ellen Fannon 44
16. *Unexpected* – Cheryl A. Paden 47
17. *The Perfect Gift* – Andrea Merrell 49
18. *Water Heaters May Quit* – Elberta Clinton
    as told to Helen L. Hoover 51
19. *Grandma's Stockings* – Bobbie Roper 54
20. *The Perfect Holiday* – Peggy Park 56
21. *Transition from Child to Teen* – Carolyn Bennett Fraiser 59
22. *God's Timing* – Alice Klies 62
23. *The Birth of Hope* – Leigh Ann Thomas 65
24. *For His Glory* – Nanette Thorsen-Snipes 70
25. *Paridoxical Peace* – Diana C. Derringer 71

26. *Child's Coat, Size 3* – Lynn Watson 73
27. *Memories of the Manger* – Beverly Hill McKinney 77
28. *Opening Doors in the Neighborhood* – Kathleen Kohler 79
29. *Significant Though Small* – Diana C. Derringer 82
30. *A Christmas Confession* – Sylvia Melvin 83
31. *Grandma's Enchanted Christmas Gifts* – Ethel Lytton 86
32. *Season's Greetings* - Lola Di Giulio De Maci 88
33. *The Jesus Tree* – Deborah Slate Ginder 90
34. *A Season of Peace* – Susan Dollyhigh 93
35. *Grief in the Celebrating* – Rebecca Carpenter 95
36. *Dear Deere Angel* – Terri Elders 97
37. *Our Thankful Time* – Dave Maynard 101
38. *The Lifesaver of My Hard Candy Christmas* – Vicki H. Moss 103
39. *Remembering the Greatest Gift* – Diana Leagh Matthews 108
40. *Foolish Question* – Yvonne Lehman 110
41. *But What If It's Dirt?* – Jeri McBryde 111
42. *The First Christmas Gift* – Norma C. Mezoe 114
43. *Return of the King* – Bob Blundell 115
44. *Timing the Lights* – Kristy Horine 119
45. *What Figure Are You?* – Linda Gilden 122
46. *Treasured Keepsakes* – Ann Brubaker Greenleaf Wirtz 126
About the Authors 128

Remembering...

Christmases... and the many stories about Christmas, considered good, bad, happy, sad, as a child, an adult, with family, with groups, alone, overworked, Santa, Jesus, traditions, poverty, plenty, receiving, giving....

My thoughts lingered for a while on the hundreds of authors who have so generously given your stories for the Moments series. This is the 14th Moments book and the 5th Christmas book.

I get emails from the authors, telling me what a blessing it is for them to share their stories. Others say someone else's life has been positively changed or strengthened. There have been family members, even entire families, that have accepted Jesus as Savior and Lord because of Moments stories. Some are used as devotions.

One of the writers, whom I see frequently, goes out of her way to seek me out, hug me, and thank me for accepting her story. She acts as if she received a wonderful gift by being able to share her story. She is the happiest giver I've ever known.

Some have said, "I don't know if you can use this article. It's not much."

Well, that depends. The widow's mite wasn't much (the smallest Roman coin; two pennies), but Jesus tells us in the Bible that he was more impressed with her gift than with the rich man's gift.

Whether light, entertaining, or serious, each story serves a purpose. When these stories are put together in a collection, and published, they become a part of world-wide giving since the royalties go to Samaritan's Purse, the organization that reaches out to the world in physical and spiritual need. They become a life-changing possibility in the moment a child, who lives in a poor country, has never received a gift, excitedly opens a shoebox.

Thank you for remembering... and sharing.

Yvonne

1

The Same Story as Last Year

Gina Stinson

A few years ago, my family attended a Live Nativity at our church. We enjoyed the crafts, good food, music and, most of all, the animals of the nativity scene. I urged my six-year-old son, Tucker, to go listen to the Christmas story being read near the stable.

He sat and listened for a few minutes and then came running toward me and said disappointedly, "Mom, they are reading the same story as last year." I chuckled and briefly explained it was because the story of Jesus' birth is the whole reason we have Christmas. He shrugged one shoulder and went on his way.

Although I was a little disappointed in his response, I knew that as we taught him more about Jesus he would come to understand the truth and the beauty of this wonderful season.

But as I mulled those words over in my head that night — "the same story as last year" — I wondered how many times I have responded the same way. *It's Christmas . . . a celebration of Jesus' Birthday . . . same story as last year. It's Christmas . . . all the hustle and bustle . . . the busyness . . . the gifts and presents . . . same as last year.* As I've listened to a sermon or read my Bible have I thought . . . *I know this story . . . Jesus, Mary and Joseph, the angels, the shepherd and wise men and the star . . . blah, blah, blah? The same old story . . . again . . . just like last year and the year before and the year before.*

Just in case you're like me and there's been a time when the story hasn't meant as much to you as it should, let's take a moment to reflect on the beauty of that night in Bethlehem over 2,000 years ago.

The no vacancy sign
The feeding trough where Jesus would lay
A fearful first time mother
The first cry of the Savior
Shepherds who heard the news first
Wise men who came from afar

Yes, I've heard the story time and time again. Yes, I can practically recite Luke 2. But what difference has that night made in my life? What do I carry with me because of the promise fulfilled in a baby? What new thing have I learned because I listened to this same story as last year?

May I never get tired of hearing the same story as last year. May the familiar words bring comfort and peace. May I be reminded of the revealed promise in a tiny baby. May my heart be humbled by the Savior who came in all lowliness and humility to save a world that would reject Him and eventually nail Him to a cross. His story doesn't get old. It may be the same one I heard last year, but it's the best story of any season.

2

A Perfect Christmas

Lana Newton

Christmas preparations always got the best of her. Some years she feared she wouldn't make it through Christmas. She joked about having a heart attack from all the stress, although she thought that wasn't totally out of the question. This year, however, she was anxious for Christmas to come.

Her oldest would be coming home with his new wife, and her second-born would be home from college. The three youngest were still at home, and she and her husband were excited about having their whole family together for the holiday. But, with the anticipation of overflowing joy came the extra stress of making sure everything would be perfect.

"Perfect," she muttered with a self-deprecating laugh. Oh, she wanted it to be. She tried. She did her best, but all her efforts never measured up to the expectations. Whether they were placed there by others or by herself, she couldn't tell. But, she felt them all the same.

She knew it would never be perfect. "After all," she reminded herself often, "we live in an imperfect world." She knew this with her head, but her heart broke each time it felt the weight of that truth. She longed for perfection, which made the inevitable failures much harder to take.

This year, she started planning early because it was so important. She made lists, planned the menu, did the shopping. She did her best to decorate their home with the familiar, yet cherished, decorations that had "decked their halls" for so many years. But, for all her planning and preparing, she still had the same stress and anxiety creep in as the day drew closer — especially with all of the last minute cleaning and baking and wrapping to do.

"There's still so much to do!" she complained to her husband, who knew what happened to his wife when this time of year came around. He'd tried to tell her many times that all that stuff didn't matter, which only succeeded in making her feel like her efforts weren't appreciated.

Everyone, she thought, *knew it did matter and was expected. He just didn't understand.*

Somehow, she made it to another Christmas Eve and fell into bed, exhausted, well after midnight. She fell asleep thinking about how she really did love Jesus. But, it bothered her so much that people don't seem to celebrate Him like they should, especially at Christmas. She didn't think long about it though, as sleep came quickly.

Before she knew it, she was back in the kitchen. She was so tired she couldn't even remember walking there. She looked around trying to decide what to do first. But, something wasn't right. Was it too early to be up? What time was it anyway? In somewhat of a daze, she thought, *I'm up now, I might as well get the turkey in the oven before everyone else gets up and wants to open presents.*

Then, she heard something from the living room. There were people in there — talking. She couldn't make out what they were saying, but it sounded like stories being told, laughter, the kind of sharing that happens so easily between people who really care about each other. She wanted desperately to go see who was there and share in the obvious fun they were having, but she couldn't move. It was as if there was an invisible chain that didn't allow her to move past her very familiar position between the stove and the kitchen sink.

She turned the oven on and started preparing the stuffing for the turkey. As she worked, she couldn't help feeling a little angry that she was stuck in the kitchen while others got to enjoy themselves. But she continued working, bitterness growing with every piece of bread she broke.

"I'm tired," she whined to herself. All the while, she kept hearing the happy commotion coming from the other room. "Why don't they at least offer to come help me so maybe later we can all sit down together and enjoy the day?"

Then, she thought she heard her name spoken from the other room. She immediately got still and heard it again. Were they calling her? Talking about her? Then, she heard a still, quiet voice saying, "You're worried about too many things. What's really important here?"

She recognized the simultaneous power and sweetness in the speaker's voice and, in the same moment, found herself on her knees with her face in her hands crying out, "I'm sorry, Lord. I know you're right. I want to spend time with you. I want to rest in you. But, there are things that need to be done . . . right?" Her question was sincere, her uncertainty obvious.

"Yes, things need to be done. But, all this?" he chided. She recognized the familiar love in his voice as he told her, "This is not why I came. I want you to know true joy that can't be taken away from you."

She sobbed into her hands as she said, "I don't know why I get so caught up in all of the other stuff when it's not important. I know this," she sputtered, "but I can't seem to get it right! I want to be with you and my family! But, I'm afraid it's too late. I've wasted so much time." She shook her head in desperation. "My kids are practically all grown." She felt a warm hand on her shoulder, then heard him say, "No, child. It's not too late. It's Christmas morning."

As the Savior's words rang in her ears, she awakened in her bed. She couldn't be sure what woke her because, at that moment, her two youngest children came running down the hall yelling, "It's Christmas morning! It's Christmas morning!"

She sat up just in time to catch them as they fell into her arms and she echoed the words, "It's Christmas morning!" As the words left her lips, she realized the hope this gave her. Christmas is all about hope. Hope in a little baby, born to save a world full of sinners. Hope that something new can be made from something old and broken. Hope for forgiveness . . . and love . . . and peace . . . and joy. Maybe this Christmas could be different. Maybe it would be perfect — if she could let go of her broken idea of what it should be.

Soon, they were all up and tearing into presents. They prayed a prayer of thanksgiving around the Christmas tree. Her husband suggested that pie wasn't really necessary since there were plenty of cookies and candy for dessert already, to which she happily agreed. She enjoyed sitting with her family and taking in the wonder of Christmas with them as she watched the joy in her children's faces.

The wrapping paper didn't get picked up right away either. In fact, the living room was a mess when the guests started arriving. The happy hostess was more at ease than her guests remembered as she greeted each one at the door and spent time sitting and talking with them through the evening. She enjoyed the fellowship with her loved ones. They played games, told stories and sang songs for Jesus into the night while dirty dishes sat scattered all over the kitchen.

It didn't matter that there was such a mess in there. It could wait, but the important things could not. And, besides, there was no one in there to see it. Not one single person. This time, Martha had chosen what was important. She and her family had celebrated Jesus — together. And, they had one of the merriest Christmases they could ever remember having.

And, she now knew why those voices seemed so distant in the middle of the night. They were words that had been spoken a long time ago in a land far away from her own. But, she welcomed the loving reminder spoken to her heart at just the perfect time . . . by a perfect Savior . . . Who was and is the perfect Gift . . . for a perfect Christmas.

> *Jesus answered and said to her, "Martha, Martha,*
> *you are worried and troubled about many things.*
> *But one thing is needed, and Mary has chosen that good part,*
> *which will not be taken away from her."*

> Luke 10:41-42

3

Here Comes Santa Claus

Phil Gladden

Recently, Ruth and I were treasure hunting on a cold Saturday morning at local yard sales. I tend to wear my favorite Santa hat this time of year as it seems to go well with the beard. You might see me sporting it anytime and anywhere throughout the month. The only exception is my wife doesn't allow me to wear it in the church.

We stopped by a small wood-framed house in the country where a yard sale sign, made from a cardboard box, had been placed near the road. Various household items were spread on blankets about the yard. Old dishes, vases and lamps of different colors and shapes, some cookbooks, old magazines, a variety of small craft items, and an old blender were an apparent attempt to make extra funds for Christmas. Although the house was somewhat isolated and in need of repair, Christmas lights surrounded the windows and various decorations were scattered around the porch. A Christmas tree was visible through the window.

As we got out of the car, an elderly lady with her two girls approached us. The girls, about five to six years of age with red hair and a healthy crop of freckles, were both absolutely adorable dressed in matching Christmas outfits. Upon our compliments, we learned that the outfits were lovingly hand-made by this woman, their grandmother. The dresses were creativity fashioned from adult men's T-shirts, tied at the waist with bright red ribbons, embordered and bedazzled with plastic jewels and trimmed with green and red felt. To the children, they might just as well have been wearing royal robes straight from the King's Palace.

The grandmother said they wanted to tell Santa their Christmas wishes. With a wink and a nod to the grandmother, I sat down on the porch and perched one child on each knee.

They were elated, and there were broad smiles on each face, but most of all, on mine. Both girls were wide-eyed with anticipation and could barely contain their excitement. The older of the two was missing a front tooth, causing her to whistle when she spoke. I told her she sounded like Mrs. Claus's tea kettle and we all broke out into hysterical laughter. The smaller child spoke less, but could not take her eyes off of my beard. She timidly tugged on it to see if it was real. I pretended it hurt yelling ouch and the laughing grew even louder.

"And what do you want for Christmas?" I asked. I listened intently to each as they told me of their various desired items, most of which were unknown to me. Still I praised them for the good choices they had made and said they must both be incredibly smart. They beamed in response.

Having dabbled in magic in the past, I performed a few simple tricks, causing a coin to jump invisibly from one hand to the other and then I made a small scarf disappear and then reappear. Their reaction far outweighed the effort, and at that moment, I was Santa Claus, in every sense of the word.

The time came to leave, and the children gave me a hug, as did the grandmother. Unknown to me, while the hugs were happening, my wife slipped an undisclosed amount of money into the jar in which the lady was keeping her change for the yard sale. An effort on my wife's part was to ensure that some, if not all, of those holiday wishes would become a reality.

We all wished each other a Merry Christmas and left with smiles and light hearts. It was a great encounter on a fantastic December day and a wonderful Christmas memory.

I would like to take a moment to thank everyone who is kind enough to read my random thoughts and ramblings. We live in a beautiful town and state to celebrate the birth of our savior. Remember, his love is what this season is all about. I hope your holiday is full of, peace, joy, and great memories. May God's blessing be with you, and your families on this holiday season.

4
A Heart Full of Questions

Kathleen Kohler

Like a thread beneath a closed doorway, faith pulled me along a path of unanswered questions throughout my childhood.

My family's assorted Christmas decorations sparked the first big inquiry. The scent of Douglass fir filled the air while we unpacked ornaments in the living room by the tree. My brother retrieved his favorite decoration from a cardboard box. Perched atop a world globe sat a silver biplane flown by none other than Santa.

But I was the one who always set out our tiny nativity set. It looked like a three-sided horse stall made of brown plastic, dusted in gold glitter. The people and animals stood no bigger than the size of my pinky. Each December when I unwrapped the set, a feeling of peace and hope swept over me.

My first attempt to push open that doorway to faith came when I asked my mom, "What does the little stall with the people have to do with Christmas?"

"It's just a thing we do," she said. Her nervous response clued me in she did not want to talk about it, or maybe she didn't know.

The second question arose during summer vacation from school.

"What religion are you?" My nine-year-old friend, Becky, asked me as she glanced over the rim of her glass of Hawaiian Punch. Janice, another friend, crunched into a Snickerdoodle and stared. I looked at the tiled kitchen floor and shuffled my feet not sure what to say.

An uncomfortable silence hung between us while my neighborhood playmates waited. Then I smiled, stood up straight, pulled back my shoulders and pronounced, "I'm Irish."

Janice gave Becky a weird look and stared back at me.

"No," Becky said. "I mean are you Baptist, or Lutheran, or Catholic?"

All words I had never heard in my nine years of living. "I don't know anything about those," I said. "All I know is, Mom's Irish and Daddy's French." They gave each other a puzzled look, shrugged, and we ran back outside to play.

The question gnawed at me all afternoon. What did Becky mean by religion?

When I returned home later that day, I asked Mom what my friends meant.

"How rude. Don't those girls have better manners?" she said. "If they ask you again, you tell them you're Episcopalian."

I stumbled over the foreign word trying to repeat it. "What's that?" I asked.

"That's what your dad's family is so you tell them you're Episcopalian," she snapped.

Startled by her response, I grew quiet and thought it best to never bring the subject up again. "Okay," I said, unsure of what I was agreeing to. And the door slammed shut on any further discussion.

My friends didn't ask me any more about religion. And with nowhere to find answers, the questions piled up in my heart.

Fall came and I went back to school, my mind occupied with fractions, world geography, and U.S. history. That is, until Halloween arrived.

Dressed like a scarecrow, I raced across my friend Lenora's yard and up onto her front porch. The house stood dark. To the left of the door a bowl of apples sat on a table with a note that read: Gone to church. Please help yourself.

I paused for a moment in the glow of a single porch light. Why didn't Lenora and her brothers dress up and trick-or-treat like the rest of the neighborhood kids? Instead, they went to church? I didn't get it. Wasn't church just for weddings and funerals?

Each question that lingered was like another swipe at a cobweb that veiled me from the truth.

The one constant was Christmas, that magical season of flying reindeer, Santa, and his elves. Each year, like welcoming an old friend, I reached into the boxes of decorations, reclaimed the wad of aged, gold-sparkled tissue paper, and unwrapped the nativity. My brother set out his flying Santa. Elves dressed in red and green felt took their usual place as sentries on the console stereo. And alone in the background sat my beloved decoration. However, it just didn't seem to fit with the rest of my family's Christmas theme.

Year after year my heart stirred with more questions about the brown plastic stall that I felt so drawn to and loved so much.

Maybe it was the couple looking at the baby, or maybe it was the animals gathered around them. I didn't know or understand the significance of the manger or the Savior it represented. I only knew how the scene made me feel and because of that I treasured it. The plastic people and animals told a story — one I wanted to know.

The mystery lived tucked away in my heart until a boyfriend invited me to church when I was in high school. I wasn't sure about all the God talk, but my curiosity piqued, so I kept going.

When Christmas came, we attended the children's program. I watched while the elementary kids took their places on the stage. The lights dimmed and a spotlight shone on a young couple. As the play continued the children formed the same scene in my nativity set. In awe, I leaned forward on my chair and listened to every child's line. It was as if the door flung open and I finally understood.

My stall was a stable, the couple was Mary and Joseph, the shepherds had received a special invitation from heaven's angels to come and worship the new baby. And the baby had a name. Jesus! The Prince of Peace, Emmanuel, God with us.

Now I knew the reason for the peace and hope that washed over my soul each year. God wanted a relationship with me — to be an active part of my life — and He was extending to me a special invitation to be His child forever.

That Christmas I accepted God's invitation. I not only discovered my faith, but years of questions were wiped away, and I finally knew the story behind my treasured Christmas decoration.

5
Wrapped in Humanity

Norma C. Mezoe

Son of God
come to earth,
royal lineage,
lowly birth.

Left angels praise
to endure our scorn;
exchanged heaven's glory,
in a manger to be born.

Wrapped himself
in the body of man;
lived on earth
to follow God's plan.

Rejected, suffered,
crucified;
laid in a borrowed tomb,
risen, glorified.

Merciful Father,
Savior Son,
Guiding Spirit,
All in One.

6
He's Always Watching

Lynn Watson

On a cold December evening, our family gathered for dinner around the shiny-chrome-and-green-Formica table. Mom, an excellent cook, served a dish ranked on the lower end of our satisfaction meter. If my six-year-old memory serves me well, she made hash. Her version included Sunday's left-over pot roast shredded and mixed with mashed potatoes. Both of those, delicious alone, combined they were a bland version of yuck my three-year-old brother and I refused to appreciate.

In our home you ate what was placed in front of you — without complaining. Part of the reasoning our parents used at the dinner table was to remind us, "Santa watches all the time. He knows everything you're doing. He is sad when boys and girls don't eat their dinner, and he makes a naughty mark by your name on his list. You don't want Santa to miss our house this year because you're not acting very nice, do you?"

So, my much older and more mature self reluctantly and silently swallowed the stuff, but Johnny chose to gag on it, spit it out, swoosh it with milk, and cry. No amount of talking, reasoning (the best you can with an unhappy toddler), or threats changed the situation. He left the table hungry. I helped Mom clean up the mess. Dad went on about his business.

A short time later I played with my dolls and Johnny pushed cars and trucks around the living room floor. Mom busied herself setting up the coffee pot for the next morning. Startled by something hitting the dining room window, Mom called to Dad. When he didn't respond, she made her way to check on the disturbance herself.

The stir roused Johnny's and my attention as well. Mom tried to hide her amusement, but her facial expression made it clear something interesting was going on outside. She motioned my brother and me to the window. Crouched next to the bushes, none other than Santa Claus, with his sack slung over one shoulder, looked up at us. We stared not believing what we were seeing. Santa frowned, raised his hand, pointed his finger, and shook it. Johnny ate every bite of every meal from then until Christmas. We both acquired a bit of healthy fear of how our behavior may affect the number of gifts under the tree.

The rest of the story:

Presents encircled the tree when we arrived home from the Christmas Eve service. It was evident Santa kept short accounts of our wrongs. My parents took advantage of this teaching moment: "Jesus also sees everything we do. When you're tempted to disobey your parents, God sees and is saddened. When you think you can get away with something, because no one else might see it or know it, God knows it. Just like Santa forgave you, God forgives our wrongs too. Because of your love for your parents and for your Heavenly Father, choosing to do the right thing is always best."

Years later we learned Dad had donned the Santa costume that night.

I remind my family of the lesson this way. "If you would be ashamed to listen to a certain song, participate in a certain activity, say certain words, be unkind, etc., with Jesus in the room, then it's best not to do it. Jesus is always in the room. He sees all we do. He loves us, and we love Him, too. Let's let our love and gratefulness for Him motivate us to choose well, set a higher standard for ourselves, and be a good example for others."

7
A First Christmas Present

Shirley Alday

Born during the great depression, Geraldine Smith never knew the fancy clothes and pretty things that some girls knew. Her clothes were hand-me-downs from her three older sisters and any toys they shared were homemade. There were five siblings older than she, and five who were younger. Maybe she felt lost in this big family, but as I reflect on the lives they lived, I think she must have felt blessed.

In 1932, she turned 13 years old and her Mom gave birth to a 12th child, my father. When Christmas came that year, her baby brother was nine months old. Although he had lots of loving family around him all the time, he had no toys.

Geraldine wanted so badly to give him something for Christmas. Each of the children would receive an orange, an apple, Brazil nuts to crack . . . and if they were lucky enough, some peppermint candy.

But babies need something special, she thought.

It is unknown where she found the gift, but for his first Christmas Russell Smith received a little ceramic wheelbarrow. The wheel did not turn. In fact, there were no moving parts. But the handles and wheel were gnawed by her baby brother as he cut his teeth. And that little two-and-a-half-inch-long wheelbarrow was pushed across the floor until the wheel was no longer round on the bottom.

Advance thirteen or fourteen years. Geraldine was married and gave birth to her first child. She named him Russell, after her younger brother. Three years later, Geraldine died in an automobile accident. Her car was filled with gifts for her baby daughter's birthday.

Geraldine was the first sibling that Russell had lost; it was a heart-wrenching time in his life. He was married and had a young family of his own. On a whatnot shelf in his home sat a tiny treasured ceramic wheelbarrow, safely out of reach of little hands.

The years brought lots of good memories of a family who loved each other and worked together to make sure each member knew they were loved.

As years passed, Russell experienced much loss. Between 1954 and 2004, twelve deaths occurred. Russell saw both parents and ten siblings laid to rest. He had only one sibling still living.

In March 2005, a devastating tornado left him and his wife, and most of their neighbors, homeless. All their personal belongings were destroyed.

Dad was now 73. It was a time when most people might have given up. But he had been raised through some hard times and he'd had people around him who had taught him that happiness isn't found in a material existence. Neighbors came to his aid, just like he would have done for them if they needed him.

He handled the whole sad situation without once breaking down. After all, he did have a lot of experience in heartbreak.

He and his wife, Lillian, started over. They cleared the place where their home had stood and built a new home.

As the family was in the yard trying to level the ground and remove debris that had been embedded by the tornado, Russell was on the tractor harrowing up the ground. While clearing the yard, I found a little trinket sticking up above the ground. As I began to clear the dirt around it, tears filled my eyes and I flagged Dad down to come and dig up what I had found. He knelt and dug like he was digging for gold. A small part was broken away and missing, but there in the dirt was the first Christmas gift he had ever received.

He cried.

Now, the broken wheelbarrow rests safely in a little box in the corner of his closet.

8
Christmas Memories

Lorilyn Roberts

I never thought roach droppings would become one of my favorite Christmas stories. But stories have a way of writing themselves on our hearts.

Each year my sister Paige invites all of us to her house. We sit around the dining room table where odd knickknacks are transformed into lovely Christmas decorations. Paige is an artist, and it's a good thing for my daughters. Most of my art projects never go as planned. I always miss an important step and my results are memorable for all the wrong reasons.

Last year all the cousins created angel ornaments to hang on our Christmas trees. The angels were dressed in white lace, had feathery wings, and a red rose dotted the front collar. Instead of halos, the kids crowned the angels with macaroni noodles.

Joy, my youngest daughter, proudly hung her angel on our tree. Christmas came and went. January rolled around, and I packed the ornaments away in our attic for another year.

This year, after I climbed up into the attic and pulled out the Christmas decorations, Joy set up the tree and I opened the first container. When I unlatched it, dozens of roach droppings littered the bottom of the box. A few tumbled out onto the living room floor. Several ornaments had brown pellets clinging to them. I was quite repulsed, only slightly less than I would have been if live roaches had scampered out.

I fetched the vacuum cleaner and vacuumed up all the droppings while visions popped in my mind of hundreds of roaches crawling over my beautiful ornaments. I cringed. Living in Florida has its dark side.

Then Joy cried out, "Mommy, my angel has no hair!"

"What happen to her hair?"

"I think the roaches ate it," Joy said.

We broke out laughing. The roaches had spent the summer feasting on the macaroni hair of my daughter's angel.

As I think back to my fondest Christmas memories, many of them are also quite eclectic. There was the year when we got trapped inside a car on fire in Manhattan. The electric windows were stuck and my grandfather smashed the driver's side window with a suitcase. Mother pulled me out through shards of broken glass. Sirens blared and emergency lights flickered in the cold night air. We never did get to see the lighting of the Christmas tree; but did spend the evening in a fancy hotel.

Later Mother told me a Hollywood director was there for a children's beauty pageant and had pleaded with her to let him take me to Hollywood. Sometimes I wonder if I missed my chance to be the next Hayley Mills (with whom I was often compared when I was young).

My most vivid memory from that snowy winter was Christmas Eve when I heard Santa's reindeer pounding on the rooftop of the apartment building. It was a loud swishing sound followed by the clatter of hoofs. I didn't believe in Santa Claus until that night. I lay in my warm bed imagining what Santa and his reindeer looked like. I wanted to jump up and peek out the window, but I was afraid if I saw them, he wouldn't leave me presents.

The next morning I ran to the window and looked below. To my surprise, there were large sleigh marks in the snow. I stared out the window for a long time.

I've thought about that more this Christmas because of a strange conversation over Thanksgiving dinner. I asked my brother's wife if their children still believed in Santa Claus. I shared my experience at my grandparents' apartment when I was young, but mentioned only the part about the sleigh tracks in the snow.

Mother said, "I saw them, too, and heard Santa land on the roof."

"You did?" I asked surprised. "I also heard the reindeer hoofs pounding on the roof. The swishing sound woke me up," I added.

Silence followed as we thought about the strange coincidence. Sometimes I wonder if God allows fanciful moments to bring comfort to children. Maybe that's what I needed at that time — to have something to believe in.

Perhaps my most poignant memory of Christmas was when I was in Vietnam to adopt Joy. Christmas music wafted through the streets of Hanoi. The beautiful lyrics filled the nighttime air. I rejoiced, so far from home, realizing nothing can silence what God proclaims from the mountaintops — or loud speakers hoisted on poles in a communist country.

Joy's hairless angel hangs on our tree this Christmas. All the gifts will be opened Christmas morning. I will eat far too much chocolate and then bemoan the five pounds I will gain. I will make my usual promise to start exercising on January 1 (and I will probably break that promise by the middle of the month). We will enjoy all the traditions that this wonderful season brings, full of joy, giving, and love.

Then the ornaments will be taken down and packed away until next year. Hopefully, the roaches will find something else to eat besides an angel's hair. Life will resume its regular course, and I will be glad for the start of a new year.

But for now, during this joyous Christmas season, I will pause to reflect on the gift of the baby, wrapped in swaddling clothes, lying in a manger, knowing someday, too, I will bow before the new-born King.

And I'm sure the angels' halos won't be made of macaroni.

9
Christmas Tradition

Lisa Braxton

After we'd put away the gifts from our October wedding, Alex broached the topic of purchasing a live tree for our first Christmas as a married couple. I eagerly agreed, embracing the idea of starting a tradition as husband and wife. I looked forward to the trip to our neighborhood garden center, strapping the tree to the top of our car, and whisking it home, like so many other couples and families.

With selections from "A Charlie Brown Christmas" playing softly in the background, I envisioned carefully removing tissue paper from around our ornaments, decorating and lighting the tree, and topping it with my African princess.

When I was single, I'd kept my holiday décor simple. I'd place the princess, who was dressed in an elegant gold robe and headdress, on my coffee table. Her confident, regal bearing and the firm hold she had on her staff inspired me to reflect on my life. Now, just as I would share my life with my husband, I'd share the princess at the top of our real tree.

I had grown up with artificial trees, as had most of my friends. Somewhere in an old photo album are Polaroids of me at the age of two or three, posed next to a silver tinsel tree. In later years, my parents purchased a series of ceiling-tall artificial evergreens that we undressed, boxed up and stored in the attic at the end of each holiday season.

Visiting the few friends who had live trees was always a teaser. I'd breathe deeply of the fresh, pine scent, and feel lightheaded and giddy.

So on that first trip to the garden center with my husband, I was brimming with enthusiasm. But I had no insight on how to choose a tree.

In our rain boots, we sloshed along the muddy rows to inspect the balsams and firs. When we'd narrowed our choices, in a romantic gesture, my husband deferred to me for the final decision.

We maneuvered a magnificent Douglas fir — which was much heavier than I'd imagined — up our condo's backstairs, down the hall, through the kitchen and into the living room. I thought we would soon be on our way to a relaxed, cozy evening on the couch admiring the unadorned tree as it absorbed water. However, once we tried to bring the tree to a standing position, we discovered a problem. It was too tall. The top branches curled against the ceiling.

I thought of a solution and told my husband to keep the tree upright as I dashed into the kitchen. In my naiveté, I came back with a pair of household scissors, thinking I could easily clip off some of the height.

My husband diplomatically suggested that we switch places, and rummaged through his utility box for a pair of pruning shears. He snipped and hacked away at the tree, leaving the top flat, but we managed to hide his handiwork pretty well with the African princess tree topper.

We skipped getting a tree the next year because we knew the mischievous kitten we had adopted would knock it down. Our tradition would need to wait.

Holiday season number three, my husband had been laid off from work. We were spending much time on his job search, trying to keep up with bills, and coming to an agonizing decision about our mischievous pet. She'd grown into an aggressive cat and had developed the nasty habit of drawing blood, clawing and biting us on a regular basis. We felt we had no choice but to have her put up for adoption at a local animal shelter. Preoccupied with handling so many challenges, we didn't pull into the garden center until a few days before Christmas. The tree inventory was sparse, reminding me of the bread aisle of a supermarket on the eve of a blizzard. The only choice we had was to pick a tree that seemed less undesirable than the other leftovers.

Our tree was large and misshapen, but we thought with some pruning by the garden center attendant, it would become acceptable. But once we got it home and lifted it upright, the unwieldy tree tumbled over, knocking down everything in its path — family photos on the entertainment center, ceramic knickknacks, and me. I was pinned, flailing under the behemoth, until my husband could free me.

When we wrestled it back into a standing position and wedged it into the plastic tree stand, the stand split apart. I was ready to give up on having a tradition, but my husband was undaunted. He made a quick trip to the local hardware store for a sturdier stand with metal bolts. On our third try we got the tree in place. Then we noticed what a monstrosity it was with one side jutting out like the bow of a ship. It leaned precariously, as if it would flip over at any moment. We decorated it anyway and told each other that it was beautiful. We were lying.

The next holiday season, the fourth year of our marriage, we shopped early, determined to get the perfect Christmas tree. My husband had found new employment. We could laugh, looking back on our adventure in cat ownership. We rationalized that the other two tree shopping expeditions were test runs. We were seasoned now. We'd know how to select the right tree.

With a confident air we strolled up and down the aisles of the garden center, carefully inspecting the Douglas firs and found one that we agreed was perfect. It wasn't as heavy as the others we'd gotten, and was much easier to get into a standing position. Securing it in the tree stand took only minutes and we loved the shape of it. It fit nicely in our living room, was symmetrical and lush. The African princess fit comfortably on top with a little clearance to spare.

We were jubilant. We'd gotten what we wanted. I couldn't wait for the neighbors to walk past the window and see our lovely tree. But when I bent down to dress the lower branches I gasped. Brown needles cascaded to the floor.

I stood back to get a better look. At least four rows of branches were dead. We asked ourselves how we hadn't noticed that at the garden center.

We had watched closely as the attendant pulled the tree from its stand, laid it on its side and wrapped it in netting. Or we thought we had. More needles fell off as my husband joined me to examine the branches. We discussed throwing the tree out and starting over. We had time. The garden center still had a decent volume of inventory left.

Then we decided not to part with it. We had fallen in love with the tree when we'd first seen it. It wouldn't have been right to abandon it. We hung ornaments and played Christmas music, committing to the tree with all of its imperfections, much as we had committed to preserving our marriage in the face of the trials and struggles during his unemployment.

We placed our most treasured ornaments on the bare branches. We added little stars, angels, and bright crosses to the lower portion. Once it was fully dressed, we decided that the dried-out branches were barely noticeable. We embraced the beauty of our not-so-perfect Christmas tree, plugged in the lights and watched it twinkle.

That's when I realized my husband and I *had* begun a Christmas tradition. And it was that, just as the African princess stood brave and courageous over an imperfect tree, my husband and I stood strong during the years of trials and financial adversity.

Most of all, despite difficulties — whether with trees or our lives — we celebrated the birth of Jesus, the only One who can bring us beauty, joy, and peace, despite imperfections and difficulties.

God remains constant regardless of the circumstances. Despite our imperfections, God wants to adorn us with his faith, hope and love.

With or without a tree, celebrating God's gifts to us is the best Christmas tradition.

10
The Gift

Helen L. Hoover

The wrapped gift sits under the tree,
With ribbon and a bow atop pretty paper.
The giver carefully chose the contents
hoping it will be cherished by the receiver.

The time arrives for the gift to be given,
handled carefully, to protect the wrapping.
Anticipation rises as the gift is brought forth.
All want to see what is wrapped so lovingly.

The wrapping is removed and laid aside,
It's the inside now that counts.
The gift is lifted for all to see.
And their appreciation mounts.

Now the receiver must make a choice.
Will the gift be placed in high esteem?
Or be rejected and put away,
never again to be seen?

As gifts come our way this Christmas,
It is our decision how we receive them.
The choice is in our hands.
The giver has done all that one can.

The gift of Jesus Christ was given long ago,
By a God who wants to help us and loves us so.
Will we accept this gift to be a part of our life,
Or set Him on the shelf and reject Him with a no?

The gifts God gave us are meant for our good.
Peace, joy, forgiveness, everlasting life, if we will accept it.
But a gift is never forced upon someone.
The choice is ours whether or not to receive it.

God so loved the world, that He gave His only begotten Son,
That whosoever believeth in Him should not perish,
but have everlasting life.

John 3:16

11

The Crocheted Angel

Sherry Diane Kitts

"Merry Christmas," store clerks tell me when I check out. I echo the greeting, but I don't feel merry. It's not the same this year and nothing seems to fit.

My husband and I moved from the mountains and snow of southwest Virginia to the Sunshine State of Florida where palm trees and shorts don't spur me on to deck the halls. Since relocating and downsizing, changes must be made in the number of things we store. So here I am sweating and pulling plastic tubs of decorations from the attic. More like work than merriment.

How can I get in the Christmas spirit?

I recall the items I need — holiday music, simmering cinnamon sticks on the stove, and my "Merry Christmas Y'all" T-shirt. A festive spark ignites my plan to sort stuff into piles of "keep," "pass on," and "toss."

I pop off the first tub lid, and an imaginary Northern chill creeps down my spine, but heat rolls from the attic opening and wafts over me, negating the feeling. I continue to bring everything down and examine the contents. The half-working twinkle lights, wise men with crushed paper crowns, and faded Santas hit the toss pile.

Why did I even bring these things here?

A box labeled "Nana" comes into view, and dried masking tape falls away as I lift it. Nana was an affectionate name our children gave their paternal grandmother. I know this box holds handmade items like her special crocheted angel. I set it aside.

Looking further, I spy a blanket of felt snow that's cushioning ornaments my mother gave our children. Two plastic babies, one in a pink nightgown and the other in blue, both with golden hangers, are asleep in fetal positions. Each year Amy and Benjy challenged one another for the top spot to place their baby on the tree.

The memory brings a chuckle as I speak to the plastic babies. "We had some happy times. You two were the kids' favorites."

My mind drifts back to the night when the kids were supposed to be asleep, and we heard the sound of something scraping across the floor. Glass ornaments began clanging, so we hurried to check on the Christmas tree. Benjy had pulled the kitchen chair close to the tree and climbed to place his blue baby higher than Amy's. He flashed a sneaky grin, proud of his accomplishment.

This year I'll pass the babies back to their original owners, knowing they'll never share a tree together again.

In another box, holly berry placemats cushion a few of the breakables. I lift one of the mats close, but no familiar scents of festivities remain. As I look at the mats, I hear the laughter of everyone gathered around to sample fudge, cookies, and treats. My mother-in-law loved everything Christmas. The day after Thanksgiving, she'd begin the preparations. The smell of fresh peppermint, chocolate sweetness, and various cookie dough flavors permeated her home and drifted outside to welcome the neighbors. Her joy of the season was contagious. We'll definitely reuse the mats, but unfortunately, my baking skills don't even compare to hers.

After much categorizing, I rejoice with the completed project until I recognize one remaining item — the Nana box I'd set aside at the beginning. Tucked in a corner and wrapped with care, sits the stunning crocheted angel. I inspect her intricate beauty. She is completely white with no facial features or markings, and her design invites admirers to form their own conceptions. The flared skirt and extended wings are held in place with a coating of stiffening solution. Through the years, she's never relaxed in proclaiming the coming of Jesus.

I recall Nana in her family room, rocking by the fireplace, chatting and laughing with friends. Her fingers moved nimbly with the crochet hooks and she only glanced down to ensure the correct chain of stitches in a row. I take some moments to reminisce about Nana's devotion to her creation.

Carrying the angel, I walk into our backyard. The gorgeous December day turns my focus to the birds' songs and their fluttering wings as they dive from trees to the feeder. A blue jay squawks his "get out of my way" order to the smaller birds. I sit and lean back into the cushioned chair, and inhale the warm air. The sharpness of the transition begins to soften. A soothing assurance eases into place.

Everyone experiences change, whether from our choices or from the constant turning of life. Change forces us to re-evaluate what's worth keeping — the items, the good memories, or a little of both. Crafted from a simple ball of string, the crocheted angel is a treasured reminder of love and joy. From the past, she's now a part of our new journey, lifting the radiance of the season and bringing hope. How can I let her go? She's definitely a keeper.

I hear music from the open window, and go inside to place her forefront on our holiday tree. I now realize that like a good dress alteration, these new Christmas adjustments fit me perfectly.

12

Operation Pony

Candy Arrington

"I'm not having a Christmas tree this year," announced the tiny, white-haired woman. "There's no reason to go to all the fuss and trouble when I'm here alone. I don't need a tree."

She turned her walker with a thump, thump, thump, as she pivoted her arthritic knees to follow. Her asthmatic breathing came in short gusts as she labored across the hardwood floor. Buried in her exhales was a slight whistle of a nameless tune to keep her mind off her pain.

Almost as an afterthought, I asked if there had ever been a Christmas in her lifetime when she asked for something she didn't received.

She looked at me, her brow crinkling in thought. "I asked for a pony once, when I was a young girl. I never got it."

"But I can get you a tree," I offered. "Or it just won't seem like Christmas."

She countered, "Christmas has never been the same since Ed died."

Giving up for the moment, I planted a kiss on her wrinkled brow and told her good-bye.

In the days that followed, I couldn't stop thinking about how sad and depressing for her to have nothing to remind her of Christmas. Without a tree, there was no designated place for gifts, and nothing to light up the dark corners of her house. I wanted to do something to brighten her life the way she had illuminated mine.

I kept coming back to the pony. She might not want a tree this year, but somewhere in her child-mind was a disappointed little girl longing for a pony. An idea began to take shape. This year the ancient little girl would have a surprise.

I needed reinforcements if my plan were to succeed. Everything had to time out perfectly.

Enlisting my father's help, we designated Christmas Eve as the appointed time. Under cover of darkness, we implemented "Operation Pony." My father visited with her in the living room while I stealthily, although not very quietly, maneuvered things into position in her dining room. I like to think she didn't know something was going on, but perhaps she only pretended for my sake.

Later, as Daddy helped her down the hall, I slid the plug into the socket. The warm glow of Christmas tree lights dispelled the gloomy darkness of the room. Beneath the tree were her gifts: a doll, a top, and a pony on wheels. While not the pony of her dreams, it was a pony all the same.

Early Christmas morning our phone rang. She never enjoyed talking on the phone, calling it "the instrument," so I was surprised to hear her voice. "I got my pony," she said simply. "And a Christmas tree, too. Thank you."

That little white-haired woman was my grandmother. My memories of her are as vivid and colorful as the beautiful patchwork quilts she made. Her influence on my life is deep and abiding, a subtle infusion of quiet hours spent together playing Chinese checkers, talking about Bible passages, and listening to stories of her childhood as she taught me how to quilt.

Whether by genetics, or by example, I know I possess her greatest strengths, and I'm thankful she celebrated one of her last Christmases on earth with a tree, a pony, and the joy of knowing how much I loved her.

13

The Falling Tree

Melissa Henderson

Raindrops pounded the roof of our truck. We should have taken the weather as a sign to turn back toward home. Wind howled while oak tree branches bounced in the air. Pools of water formed on the side of the road.

Did those things stop our family from venturing out to the local tree farm in search of the best Christmas tree? No. Not rain, wind or mud would prevent us from choosing the best tree.

Onward we went, turning on the gravel road leading to the designated field for parking. Thick mud stuck to the wheels of our small pickup truck. We were not going to let a little weather bother us.

After all, we'd had experience with bad weather at Christmas-tree-choosing-time in past years. We had traveled through snow, pouring rain, wind, and freezing temperatures. One peculiar weather year the temperature was hot instead of normal winter cold.

We'd worn coats, hats, gloves and scarves to pick out a tree. We'd also worn shorts and short sleeved shirts the year with warm weather.

A little rain would not prevent us from the yearly tradition of riding the wagon to the tree field, picking out the best tree and cutting it down.

This year would be wonderful even with rain and wind.

Following our usual routine, we enjoyed the wagon ride, walked rows and rows of trees before finding the perfect tree. We finally chose the biggest tree we could find. Success!

When the tree was cut and loaded on the wagon we positioned ourselves for the ride back to the barn. Hot cider and cookies waited for everyone.

A great day!

The eight foot tall and very round pine tree was loaded into the back of our pickup truck. Deciding the tree would stay put, we didn't bother to secure it with ropes or twine.

Waving goodbye to the tree farm helpers, we headed home. Rain had stopped and the weather was quiet.

The huge tree remained still. Then, we reached highway speed.

As fast as the blink of an eye, we glanced back and saw our beautiful tree lift up and shoot like like an arrow out of the truck bed.

Good thing no one was behind us. The road was empty except for us and the tree.

My husband slowed the truck and pulled to the side of the road. He and our son ran as fast as their legs would carry them and retrieved the tree from the middle of the highway.

They lifted the tree into the truck bed and this time they used twine and rope to make sure the big tree would not try to escape again.

After arriving home, we followed the usual list of ways to care for the freshly cut tree. Shake it outside, trim the lower branches and place the tree in a stand before bringing inside. Add water once the tree is secured.

Easy and done with a quick pace.

Finding the right spot in the corner of the living room, we positioned the tree with the best side facing forward. Decorating was next. Boxes of old and new ornaments were brought out from storage. Colored lights were strung and more white lights were added. Each decoration provided opportunity for sharing old memories and making new ones.

By late evening the tree was decorated. A sight to behold. Beautiful.

Finally, time for sleep.

Crash! Pop!

Sounds of shattering ornaments filled the quiet night. Awakened by these strange sounds, we ran from our bedrooms to the living room.

What a sight! The tree had fallen and ornaments were broken and scattered across the floor.

After sweeping glass and making sure all sharp pieces were placed in the trash, we felt safe enough to try to sleep again. All was fine for the night.

The next night, we were again awakened by the tree falling. More ornaments broken. More mess to clean.

Why was the tree falling during the night and not during the day? We had no answer. We only knew we were running out of ornaments and lights.

Attaching the tree to the wall with a bungee cord and a nail seemed to be the answer.

After searching the tool box and working on the wall and the tree, my husband assured me the tree would not move until after Christmas when we were ready to take it down.

Yes, the tree stayed safely in place. No more broken ornaments.

We learned valuable lessons with this falling tree. Do we always have to choose the biggest of everything? Does the size of a tree make Christmas any different? Were we focusing on the right part of Christmas?

While pondering these questions, we paused and remembered the true meaning of Christmas.

The celebration of the birth of Jesus is the big thing, the true reason for the season. Not the biggest tree or the most ornaments. Our family time together at the tree farm gave us wonderful memories. We could choose a small tree and all would be well.

The next Christmas, we found a smaller tree and enjoyed the blessing of sleeping through the night without worrying about a falling tree.

Merry Christmas!

14
Noel Reflections

Lydia E. Harris

After Christmas, I finally found time to take our car in for its required service. Since the work could take several hours, the dealer provided shuttle transportation back to my home.

"Do you like your job?" I asked the van driver.

"It's all right," he said. "I'm seventy-seven, and it gives me something to get up for each morning."

Wishing he had a greater purpose for getting up each day, I prayed God would touch his heart and give his life meaning.

When he dropped me off at my home, he handed me his business card. I glanced at the card. "Noel. What a nice name."

I thanked him and went inside.

Later that day, when Noel picked me up, I climbed into the back seat of the van and handed him a couple of homemade peanut butter cookies.

"Thank you," he said, and ate them right away.

"Noel, you have the perfect name for Christmas," I said. "How was your Christmas?"

He replied, "Fine. But I'm glad it's over."

"Because of all the activity?" I asked.

"Kind of," he said. "My birthday is on Christmas Day."

I commented that his birth must have been a wonderful Christmas gift to his family and mentioned carols with the words Noel, Noel. But he remained quiet. I was hoping to talk to him about Jesus, the real Gift of Christmas, but I didn't sense interest. So I dropped the subject and wondered how a person who shares a birthday with Jesus would not want to talk about that.

However, as I thought further, and didn't know exactly why Noel felt relieved that Christmas was past, I realized I could relate. To my surprise, I had just said the same thing to my husband. Normally, I love everything about Christmas and wish it could last longer. But multiple medical appointments throughout the season had blurred my focus, and I didn't decorate our usual Christmas tree. Although I was glad the outward trappings of the holidays were over, I felt disappointed that inwardly I had somehow missed Christmas.

Even though I felt that way then, I realized all was not lost. I can celebrate Christmas in my heart — not on one day only, but all year. I don't need festive decorations or special parties and activities. I simply need a quiet heart and time to worship the Babe of Bethlehem, who grew up, died for my sins, rose from the dead, and will soon return as the conquering King.

As I pray, read my Bible, and reflect on the true Gift of Christmas, its meaning will linger in my heart all through the year. So I'll continue to sing the lyrics to "The First Noel." And as I do, I'll pray for my van driver, Noel.

Ideas to Celebrate Christmas All Year:
- Read through the Christmas cards, perhaps one each day, and pray for those who sent them.
- Keep favorite Christmas books and stories handy to read throughout the year.
- Play joyful, uplifting Christmas carols at any time, and sing along.
- Light a candle and reflect on Scriptures about Jesus' birth. (See Luke 1:26–38; Luke 2; Matthew 1:20–25; and Matthew 2.)
- Pray for a worshipping, seeking heart like the wise men had.
- Follow the shepherds' example, and eagerly share the Good News of Jesus with others.
- Like the angels did, glorify God by words and actions.
- Ask, "Whom can I bless today?"

15

Just One More Child

Ellen Fannon

Her motto is, "Just one more child."
This is what the shoebox lady, Elaine Lauderdale, has on her mind when she encourages everyone to participate in Operation Christmas Child at Rosemont Baptist Church in Niceville, Florida. Rosemont, a small church with an average attendance of approximately seventy people on Sunday morning, has sent out over 600 Christmas shoeboxes a year for the last several years.

Last year, December 2018, the total was 714. Elaine spearheads this effort through her unique concept of mass production of shoeboxes. Throughout the year, she hunts for bargains and buys items in bulk to go in shoeboxes. This system makes boxes affordable to produce. Because items are purchased throughout the year, Rosemont realized that Elaine needed her own place where she could organize and store items until time to pack boxes in the fall — hence the "Shoebox Room" was born.

Elaine, along with her longtime friend and fellow shoebox fanatic, Mary Kirkland, spend countless hours sorting, counting, and organizing items so that by the time the actual packing takes place, everything is ready to go. Usually in October, there are several shoebox packing parties. Last year, for the first time, Rosemont had help from students at Rocky Bayou Christian School in Niceville who were completing community service hours, as well as help from several people outside the church.

This year marks the twenty-sixth anniversary of Operation Christmas Child, a project of Samaritan's Purse, which uses gift-filled shoeboxes to demonstrate God's love in a tangible way to children in need around the world. The boxes are filled with small toys, personal hygiene items, school supplies, clothing, and other goodies, and delivered to impoverished children around the world. For many of these children it is the first gift they have ever received.

Since 1993, Operation Christmas Child has collected and delivered more than 157 million shoebox gifts to children in more than 160 countries and territories. It is not the goal of Operation Christmas Child to supply children with a lifetime of soap, toys, or school items. In fact, a child can only receive one shoebox in his/her life. Rather, it is an opportunity to share about the love of Jesus. Since 2010, more than 14 million children who have received a shoebox gift have participated in The Greatest Journey — a 12-lesson discipleship program.

From trained, local volunteers children learn what it means to follow Jesus and share their faith with friends and family. It is estimated that for every three shoeboxes sent out, one child comes to know Jesus as Lord and Savior. That estimate doesn't include family members or others in their towns and villages who may also come to a saving knowledge of Jesus Christ as the result of their child receiving a simple gift of love. The testimonies of children whose lives have been forever changed by that one simple act of love are inspiring — from a child receiving *exactly* what is needed, to carefully counted shoeboxes being multiplied when more children were present than boxes.

This is what drives Elaine to pack just one more box for one more child. Immediately after the shoebox dedication day, the second Sunday in November, the shelves in the shoebox room are bare. Elaine starts again, after Christmas, looking for bargains. People all over town know Elaine and Mary, and they have recruited many of them to help. Discount stores call when items go on sale. Each month she asks the church members to supply something — soap month, yoyo month, pencil month, etc. The expense, spread over the entire year among several people, is minimal.

Many people, both inside and outside the church, make items to go in the boxes, such as dresses, crocheted hats/scarves, tote bags, doll clothes and blankets, or put together sewing kits, and fishing supplies. Rosemont set up a shoebox fund for people who want to contribute money in addition to, or instead of buying items. Elaine and Mary use this fund to purchase extra things needed to fill the boxes. And Elaine makes sure they are full. She has taught all the packers how to utilize every square inch of those boxes.

But most important is prayer. During every packing session, Elaine stops, gives a "mini sermon," as she is never at a loss for words, and prays over the boxes and the children who will be receiving them.

Other churches, many much larger than Rosemont, have sent their shoebox coordinators to learn from Elaine. Most churches that participate in Operation Christmas Child encourage members to take home and pack a box or two. Elaine does this, as well. Even though massive numbers of boxes emerge from the shoebox room, members of the congregation are highly encouraged to take home and pack their own personal boxes. Of the 714 boxes sent from Rosemont last year, 65 were packed by individuals or families. Several people have received thank you notes or emails from the child who received their box.

Elaine's name is well known in the southeastern region with Atlanta as the Operation Christmas Child processing center. She and Mary, as well as other church members, have traveled to Atlanta many times to volunteer for several days working in the processing center. Elaine would be the first to tell people that she doesn't accomplish putting together the massive number of shoeboxes all by herself or even with Mary. She gives all the credit to God. But it is her infectious passion and enthusiasm for shoeboxes that excites everyone around her and makes them want to get in on the action. Her vision and leadership have enabled a small church to do the impossible — sending out 714 boxes. That's why she's called the shoebox lady and that's why her vision has become Rosemont's vision of "just one more child."

16

Unexpected

Cheryl A. Paden

In December of 1987 I was eight months pregnant and expecting my third child the end of January. Being pregnant and hearing the Advent story, I could easily imagine what Mary must have felt like. It made the story seem more real. I could imagine Mary visibly pregnant, the swollen ankles, the backache, and the tiredness. But to my surprise, the story took on a deeper meaning for me that year.

December 23rd I stayed up late to fill the stockings, wrap the last gift, and finish the food for our Christmas celebration. With only few hours of sleep I woke early on the 24th to celebrate Christmas with our own little family. It was a long day with a three and five year old as I finished the preparations for gatherings with our extended family. We concluded the day with midnight Christmas Eve worship. We arrived home, slept six hours and drove to my in-laws on Christmas day.

That night we returned home again, unloaded the car, and got the children to bed. Every muscle and joint of my body ached. I crawled into bed and put my head on the pillow just long enough to close my eyes. Less then an hour later, I woke my husband with the words, "Honey, we need to go to the hospital."

We checked in and waited through the night, and into the next day, for our son to arrive. At 30 P.M. on the 26th our son, Aaron, was born. Because he was premature and having trouble breathing he was life-flighted to the neonatal intensive care unit (NICU) at the University Med Center in a city an hour from our home. Driving in an ice storm, we joined our son for another sleepless night.

This was not the joyful delivery I had expected to experience. Not only that, I had sold all my baby things at a garage sale and was waiting until January to set up the nursery. We had no crib, no bassinet, no baby swing, no stroller — nothing. We were totally unprepared. It wasn't supposed to be like this. I had followed all the doctors' orders, taken my prenatal vitamins, and eaten healthy food.

The experience made Mary's story become more real for me. After an angel's visit, Mary was unmarried and pregnant. She faced the possibility of public disgrace, loss of her fiance's love, her pending marriage, and the loss of home and family desired by a young Jewish girl. That is not how Mary expected her life to be. Later, she gave birth in a distant town, with nowhere to lay her newborn, except in a manger.

Scripture reveals that Mary trusted in God's plan. *"I am the Lord's servant," Mary answered, "May it be to me as you have said"* (Luke 1:38 NIV).

She not only trusted, she rejoiced. *Mary said, "My soul glorifies the Lord and my spirit rejoices in God my Savior"* (Luke 1:46 NIV).

She carefully thought about her situation. *"Mary treasured up all these things and pondered them in her heart"* (Luke 2:19 NIV).

Our newborn came at an unexpected and unplanned time in our family. But he soon became a happy healthy baby and grew into a fine young man.

More unexpected circumstances came as time went by, and my life does not always so the way I planned, but I choose to respond like Mary. I can trust in God's plan for me, rejoice in all circumstances, and ponder his blessings for me.

That was a Christmas to touch my heart, understand Mary, and appreciate the birth of Christ in a much deeper way.

17

The Perfect Gift

Andrea Merrell

*Every good and perfect gift is from above,
coming down from the Father of the heavenly lights,
who does not change like shifting shadows.*

James 1:17 NIV

A yummy brunch prepared by my talented husband on Christmas day has become our typical holiday tradition. For the five granddaughters, age ten and under, food was the last thing on their minds. While seated at the table, they giggled as they kept cutting curious, anxious glances toward the brightly wrapped gifts snuggled under the tree.

When brunch was finished and most of the mess put away, we all settled in the living room while my daughter handed out the gifts. My youngest granddaughter reached out for her first one from me and her grandpa. She excitedly tore into the colorful paper and ripped it to shreds to see what was inside.

This four year old was expecting the special doll she had requested. My heart threatened to shatter as I watched her eyes narrow and her shoulders droop in disappointment when she saw a variety of clothes inside the box. She didn't say a word, but she didn't have to. Her countenance and body language said it all. She simply looked around the room at each face, then dropped her little head to hide the tears.

Before her emotions could escalate out of control to a full-blown meltdown, I quickly grabbed another box and placed it in her hands. She raised her head and gazed at me expectantly, her hope restored. This time she carefully pulled the paper away piece by piece as if afraid to be let down again. When her eyes rested on the doll she had asked for, a huge grin spread across her face. She jumped up, danced around, and squealed in delight.

Reflecting on her reaction this particular Christmas day made me wonder how many times God has given me a gift and watched as my countenance fell because of my disappointment. Maybe the gift wasn't exactly what I had asked for or wanted. Did I hang my head to hide the tears? Did I break His heart with my reaction?

The Bible tells us *every good and perfect gift is from above*. What I've learned over a lifetime of serving God is that He always knows what's best for us and exactly what we need — and *when* we need it. The good news is He also promises to give us the desires of our heart when we delight in Him. But sometimes we have to wait. At other times, the gift He gives is so much better than the one we requested.

God is the giver of all good gifts, and His gifts are always delivered right on time. His time. And they are most definitely worth waiting for.

During this Christmas season, step away from the busyness of the holiday, and spend some time with Jesus — the greatest gift of all time. *Take delight in the LORD, and he will give you the desires of your heart* (Psalm 37:4 NIV).

18
Water Heaters May Quit

Elberta Clinton as told to Helen L. Hoover

After taking a shower and getting ready for church, I told my husband, "Joe, only lukewarm water came out of the faucet. Do you suppose our water heater quit?"

"I'll check and see." He headed down into the basement.

Hmm this could put a hitch on the cookie making time this afternoon.

Joe soon returned. "Sorry, honey, the water heater has quit."

"Well, I guess I'll need to dig out my large pans to heat water."

Heating water was something I knew about from my childhood. Maybe this would be a learning experience for the grandkids.

After getting back home from church and fixing lunch, I began to get out the mixing bowls, flour, sugar and other supplies needed for making cookies — plus the big pans for water.

Only three of our eight grandchildren would be able to come this year. They ranged in ages from six to eighteen and were busy with varied activities. I was glad some of them could still come and evidently enjoy themselves. When I sent out a text asking if they wanted to come, fifteen-year-old Anna and seventeen-year-old Rachel both replied, "Why wouldn't we want to come?"

That certainly warms a grandmother's heart.

For fifteen years, Joe and I have hosted an afternoon of making Christmas cookies with the grandkids. It's a fun time, as they mix, bake, taste and share with each other. Four or five different kinds of cookies are made. Enough of the cookie dough is baked for everyone to have several cookies and the rest of the dough is made into balls, frozen, and sent home with the youngsters for future baking. Not having hot water for clean-up could make this year a little different.

"What are you doing with all the pans on the stove, Mimi?" Six-year-old Phoebe asked when she arrived.

"Our water heater quit, so I'm heating water. This is the way I had hot water as a child. My mother heated water in pans and then diluted it to the right temperature with cold water."

Her eyes widened. "Wow, can I see?"

"Ok, but don't touch."

As I held her up, she commented, "Look at all that steam."

Measuring, mixing and baking started taking place in earnest. Lack of hot water didn't seem to bother anyone.

As I grew up, my mother had impressed upon me, "If you can't get what you want, make do with what you've got." That's what we did.

Soon the afternoon was over, cookies were wrapped and sent home with the youngsters, the kitchen cleaned, and the floor swept.

"Joe, who do you suggest we call about fixing our water heater?"

"I don't know who is reliable. How about calling your friend Sandi to ask her husband. He usually knows about local repairmen."

Sure enough, he had a couple suggestions. Sandi said, "Steve, the grandson of deceased church members Emma and David, works at the shop downtown."

Hmm, our church members had prepared meals for David for three months while he was on hospice care at a daughter's home. David had been concerned about his grandson who was struggling with life and finances. David and I had prayed about Steve. That was three years ago and I wondered how the grandson was doing now.

Joe and I decided to call the downtown repair shop since they had given this young man a job, although I didn't expect to see him. When I called Monday morning, it was a pleasant surprise when they said a repairman would be out in the afternoon.

The repairman arrived on time, was very courteous, and seemed competent with the water heater. He mentioned to Joe that he was buying a home and getting married soon. It sounded like this young man was doing well.

When the repair was done, he asked how we found out about the shop. I told him that Sandi and her husband had made the recommendation.

"How do you know them?" he asked

"We go to the same church."

"Oh, then you probably knew my grandparents, Emma and David."

"Yes, we did. Are you Steve?"

"I am. It was nice of the church people to prepare meals for my grandfather during the time he was sick. It made it easier for my aunt. And your pastor was kind and considerate at the funeral."

"We were happy to help," I said, and Joe nodded.

As Steve left, my heart overflowed with thankfulness to God for sending him to do the repair job. It was a blessing to know that Steve was doing well now. His grandfather would be pleased. And it was apparent the church's kindness to David had affected Steve, too.

As I reflected on the problem with the water heater, I realized it produced wonderful results. The time with the grandkids wasn't disrupted. I got to explain about how I had hot water as a child. But the best was learning that Steve is now a respected repairman and a kind young man.

Water heaters may quit, but God never does. That was certainly the start of a wonderful Christmas season.

19

Grandma's Stockings

Bobbie Roper

If you looked in on the Otto family on Christmas morning in the 1960s, you would find us driving to Grandpa and Grandma's house. No Christmas card was more beautiful than rural, western New York. It truly was a winter wonderland of snow-covered trees, brisk winter winds, snowflakes blowing across the landscape, and ice-covered ponds sparkling in the sun. The drive was beautiful.

As we turned into their long driveway, we'd see a pond on the left, and a little further down, the old wooden bridge. The clanking of the tires on the boards was a little scary, but we always made it across. Around the curve, down a little hill, and there sat Grandma's rose garden, covered in snow. The house stood directly ahead with its wide porch that overlooked another pond. How I loved this place not only for summer vacation but especially at Christmas time.

The smoke coming from the chimney was the first scent to greet us. Then the smell of turkey and pumpkin pie filled the air as Grandpa opened the front door. Snow-covered boots were left inside the front door. After hugs, we rushed to the living room where a fire crackled in the fireplace and stockings hung from the mantel. There were six of them with names at the top. Four for my siblings and me, and two for my cousins. The rule was that we couldn't look in the stockings till everyone arrived. And the cousins were always late. The waiting was awful!

When they finally arrived and hellos were said, Grandma carefully took down each stocking and handed them out. It didn't take me many years to figure out that these stockings were not hung by Santa because we already got his stockings at home. I also realized that Grandma's stockings were so much cooler than Santa's!

These contained lead pencils and notebooks, coloring and activity books, crayons, colored pencils, hand-held games, little dolls and hair accessories for the girls, cars and trucks for the boys, rubber balls and jacks, balloons, paddle balls, jump ropes, candies, gum, nuts, and — always in the toe of the stocking — an apple and an orange.

I wondered how Grandma could pack so much stuff into one stocking. She really knew how to make her grandkids smile. She also knew how to keep us entertained until Christmas dinner was served.

That was nearly sixty years ago, but the memories are still sweet. Thank you, Grandma, for always making Christmas special! Your stockings were the best!

20

The Perfect Holiday

Peggy Park

Most of the women I know are exhausted each year with all the Christmas preparations. We put expectations on ourselves for the *perfect* holiday. So how do we deal with this and keep Christ in Christmas?

Jesus said He is the prince of peace. *"Peace I leave with you, My peace, I give to you"* (John 14:27). So where does that peace go when we frantically run to and fro, buying, wrapping, cooking, mailing?

I have discovered several ways to help me slow down and celebrate the message of Christmas.

The most important way I've found to keep Christ central is to come to Him first thing each day to fellowship with Him, worship and adore him, read His word and lay my burdens at His feet.

Proverbs 10:27-29 tells us reverence for God adds hours to each day. We will find this scripture to be true as we take even a short time to focus on Him before we begin our day. If we have holiday guests, we may need to set the alarm a little early to allow for this before they begin to stir.

When our children were growing up we drew names (the five of us) for what we called Christmas angels. The point was to do nice things in secret for the person whose name was drawn. It might involve making their bed, leaving a treat on their pillow, or doing a chore that would have been theirs to do. It was a lot of fun when we learned who our secret angel was and it helped the children learn to serve others. When the angel was revealed on Christmas morning there were squeals of, "That was you?" The result was it helped us to remember the example of Jesus as He served others, and we talked about the true meaning of Christmas.

Now, our immediate family includes eight adults and six grandchildren so we have adopted my birth family's habit of drawing names, which makes gift selection a lot simpler and a big relief for all of us. My daughter, Susan, has assumed the responsibility of drawing the names for each adult as we are in different states. Each of the three families do not come home for the holidays every year so some mailing is involved unless we buy online and have them delivered.

In the last couple years, we decided to have the children draw among themselves which has worked great and reduces the number of gifts the children receive. Each one can give thought to the gift for the name drawn. This has reduced the dilemma of gift selection and has made it a joy instead of having a long list to work through.

Another way I've found to reduce the pressure is to focus on my close friends' birthdays throughout the year rather than trying to get each a Christmas gift. When I come across something in my shopping that seems perfect for a particular friend I get it. But we don't feel pressured to exchange gifts. We celebrate our birthdays with lunch, a small gift, or just a carefully selected card.

An important part of my Christmas celebration is serving someone in need, financially or relationally, as I remember Matthew 25:40: *"The king will reply, Truly I tell you, whatever you did for one of the least of these brothers and sister of mine you did for me."*

For one family in particular, I make little goodie-bags for each of the four children and the parents because they do not have an involved extended family. The mother suggests items to go with the sweet treats. Then I invite them to my home a couple weeks before Christmas Day. I give them the bags, we have cookies and lemonade and catch up with the happenings in their lives. The four teens are getting beyond little trinkets, so this year I now give them gift cards and — at their mother's suggestion — several of my published devotions and a story about my birth family's Christmas traditions.

A family I have befriended over the years has Christmas celebrations. So it's like Christmas all over again when I show up with cookies or other treats in January or February.

I make a menu for the week when family will visit. I've found that store-bought pies are sometimes better than some I made. I also avail myself of some already-prepared foods and delegate some of the food preparations to the children who are here at Christmas. Delegating food preparation gives me more time to reflect on the meaning of the holiday.

Our son-in-law, Craig, introduced us to the practice of having a birthday cake for Jesus on Christmas Eve. This helps the children remember what the celebration is all about as we sing "Happy Birthday Jesus." After our supper and the cake, we proceed to the living room to sing carols. It was a joyful day for me when I found a copy of the Christmas storybook I had as a child. I bought it and reading it to the younger grandchildren has become a part of our celebration.

I guard against thinking I have to attend every church or community event designed to celebrate Christ's birth. Too many activities drain my energy, leaving me little time for reflection on the wonderful advent. However, I find meaning in the church's candlelight Christmas service.

I have learned to lay aside my expectations of the *perfect* holiday, slow down, and be sure my activities do not usurp my time to be with, celebrate, and worship the Birthday Baby, Jesus.

21

Transition from Child to Teen

Carolyn Bennett Fraiser

One month after my thirteenth birthday, I found out my daddy's long-awaited job transfer had been approved. He was expected to begin work right after the New Year, so he would need to leave before Christmas. But we had one big problem: We needed to sell our house.

As Christmas approached, the house remained unsold. I knew what that meant. Daddy would leave us behind, and Christmas was not going to be the same.

Christmases had always been magical for me. Bright lights sparkled in the neighborhood. Colorful gifts multiplied under the tree as the date approached. The aroma of cookies and bread filled the house as my mom prepared for our annual family dinner. Although temperatures in southern Florida could easily climb into the 80s in December, my dad always had a fire ready in our fireplace, roaring in anticipation of the morning. Christmas was my favorite time of the year. It even trumped my birthday in November.

As soon as the sugar rush from Halloween abated, the magic of Christmas began to grow. By the time my dad unpacked the floor-to-ceiling Christmas tree in early December, I could barely contain myself. Every year, our family decorated the tree together. Each ornament carried memories of Christmases past: retro balls from the year we spent at Grandma's, Hallmark collectibles, angels and snowflakes. I didn't care that our tree wasn't themed and that all the decorations created a hodgepodge. The tree represented thirteen years of memories that grew larger each year.

But this year, Dad wouldn't be there to pack up the tree and decorations so Mom decided to keep the holiday simple. Instead of our large Christmas tree, Dad brought down only the small treetop. Mom placed it in a basket of pine cones. The lights, garland, and our beloved ornaments would remain packed for the upcoming move — whenever that might be. Each time I looked at our tree, it was a harsh reminder. Daddy was leaving, and we didn't know when we could join him. It could be a few weeks or a year. But he was leaving.

One afternoon, my sister and I arrived home from school to the aroma of popcorn. Since Mom didn't allow us to have snacks before dinner, we looked at each other and shrugged. With a string and needle in hand, she led us to the family room — where our small tree sat dwarfed by the fireplace — to teach us how to string popcorn and cranberries to create a natural, homemade garland for the tree.

"I don't want to." I pouted. None of this was fair. I stuffed the rest of my brooding deep inside myself.

"Just try it," Mom said. "It will be fun."

Within a half hour, pieces of broken popcorn littered the floor. "Oops, there goes another piece." My sister laughed as she picked up the popped kernel and tossed it into her mouth.

As we strung the popcorn string around the tree, it didn't look as empty as before and something about it glowed just a little.

When Christmas morning arrived, for the first time in my life, I was not excited as Mom knocked on my door.

I moaned and pulled the sheets over my head.

"Come on. It's Christmas!" She shook the covers, but I only buried myself deeper until, after more encouragement, I pulled myself out of bed. But the magic was gone.

Walking down the hall, I could smell waffles, a holiday special. But I didn't want any of it. I didn't want my dad to leave. I didn't want to move away from my home and friends. I wanted to turn back the clock to another Christmas morning, when I felt the magic.

As I walked through the kitchen into the family room, Christmas music floated through the air. The fireplace was alive with fire. Our stockings were filled with gifts, and presents crowded around the little tree. Mom and Dad had done their best to make Christmas seem as normal as possible.

I went through the motions of Christmas morning, but none of it mattered. I didn't care what was under the tree or in our stockings. I didn't want anything except my daddy. I wanted him to stay.

Looking back, the three months we were apart doesn't seem like a long time, but it did when I was thirteen. That year, I walked through a passageway between childhood and adulthood. Perhaps I reacted in an immature way, but perhaps it was a growing awareness that loved ones may not always be with us.

Although I knew I could never return to the innocent childhood fantasies of Christmas morning, I never again took for granted the years we are together. Now, there is a different kind of special — more magical than colorful gifts, bright lights, and even a roaring fireplace. While the gifts are still fun to open, they are overshadowed by something else.

I learned to have a greater appreciation of family — whether they are the ones who surround me or they're no longer with me — especially at Christmas.

22

God's Timing

Alice Klies

"All I want for Christmas is a horse."
I never wished for my two front teeth, although the gaping hole brought laughter when I smiled. Nope, every Christmas Eve, from the time I turned six, I wished on stars and prayed for a horse. Not just any horse. I wanted a white Arabian stallion, one with a silver mane and tail, just like the picture I tore out of a magazine while my mom and I sat in a doctor's waiting room.

I plastered the walls in my bedroom with pictures of horses. I taped a poster of a big black Friesian horse above my bed. Just imagining the power in the Friesian breed made tiny goose bumps rise on my forearms. I imagined riding on his back with my arms outstretched while embracing the wind in my face. The picture of an enormous black and white Gypsy horse, with its shaggy white feet took priority in a frame on my dresser.

I wrote stories about horses and drew pictures of them. Through my fantasy world of wishing and praying to own a horse, my nighttime dreams fulfilled a satisfaction that one munched on grass in my backyard. Bedtime prayers always ended with, "Please God, all I've ever asked for is a horse. Please? Amen."

My favorite movies were westerns. I sat spellbound in the movie theater on Saturday mornings. I didn't care so much about the Lone Ranger, but I sure loved hearing, "Hi-Ho, Silver." When the Lone Ranger shouted, "Hi-Ho, Silver," Silver reared on his hind legs and rushed to save the hero.

Roy Rogers rode a golden Palomino named Trigger who sported a white mane and tail. Gold seemed to glitter from his coat, not to mention that he performed more tricks than a magician. The chase scenes with the spotted Indian ponies racing over mountain ranges often brought me to tears when one of the ponies stumbled and fell, or worse, took a bullet and lay still on the screen.

Every book about a horse that graced my three-foot bookcase, had tattered corners from the many times I read them. I had to tape the front and back covers of my favorite book, *Black Beauty*. I could never read through it without a box of tissues at my side. Thank goodness it had a happy ending!

And so, Christmas came and went for twenty-nine years. A horse never appeared under my Christmas tree, or in my backyard. The best I could do in all those years was to muck stables as a teenager to get the privilege of riding the stable rental horses, and later on, I attended every Arabian horse show that came to Scottsdale, Arizona. I kept dreaming, praying and wishing on stars.

In November of 1978, I taught tennis at a resort nestled in the heart of Scottsdale. A woman approached me one afternoon in the tennis shop. She held the hand of a little boy.

"Good morning, " she said. "I have a proposition for you. A friend told me that you have always wanted a horse. How would you like to give my son lessons and we can barter. In exchange for tennis lessons, I will give you an Arabian foal that one of our mares is expecting any day now. Would that work for you?"

When she spoke the last sentence, I choked on my saliva. After surviving the shock, I stuttered, "I… I don't know what to say. I don't have a place to keep a horse, much less feed it."

 "No problem," she replied. "We will keep him at our ranch and feed him. We have our own tennis court, so you can teach my son there and then visit with your foal anytime."

My hands shook as I covered my face with them. We spent the next hour talking about the details, including the wonderful friend who had made this connection. The woman explained that the colt (or filly), because of genetics, would be born dark grey, but as it matured would turn snow white and likely have a silver mane and tail.

That night I pulled out a box of childhood memories. I smoothed the wrinkles out of a rumpled picture of a white Arabian stallion. I rubbed my fingers over the tattered *Black Beauty* book as tears ran down my cheeks. I looked up. "Thank you, God. Merry Christmas."

The mare delivered a colt, which turned snow white in four years, had a flowing silver mane and tail and became my heart and soul and friend for twenty-two years. I often sat on his back and rode him with my arms outstretched in joyful wonder with the wind in my face. I also landed a marketing job with one of the largest Arabian breeding farms and spent seven years among hundreds of horses.

Every now and then, dreams and wishes come true. God's timing for answering prayer isn't always in tune with ours.

23
The Birth of Hope

Leigh Ann Thomas

He doesn't even know me.

I brushed my hand over my husband's forehead. His skin was cold and clammy against my fingertips. His eyes, wild and unfocused. My heart squeezed and a sense of panic challenged my efforts to stay calm.

Lord, what is happening?

I inhaled and blew a slow breath, disoriented from the emergency room chaos — a blend of medical jargon, bright lights, and strange alarms. A doctor and multiple nurses moved like faceless blurs as they asked me to step back and let them do their jobs.

Stepping away from the man I'd loved for over twenty years seemed wrong. As if the separation of a few feet could morph into a distance from which we might never recover.

Lord, I don't understand.

Two hours before, my younger daughters and I had scrambled for coats and shoes as we waited for my husband, Roy, to arrive home from work. The kitchen clock read 5:20 P.M. and my heart waited for the sound I treasured — my sweetheart's footsteps as he entered the back door of our rural home in central North Carolina.

After a hectic week of work and school, we were eager to jumpstart our Christmas vacation with dinner out and time together as a family. Our oldest daughter had to work, but she would join us later in the evening for movie time at home.

The clock ticked to 5:40 P.M. and still no sound of footsteps. *Why hasn't he called to say he's running late?* When I called to remind him of our plans, the line clicked as if someone answered but there was no sound.

On the next try, he answered. "Listen to me. I need you to listen to me . . . " His voice sounded strange, otherworldly.

"Honey? Where are you? What's wrong?"

"I've been in an accident." His words trailed away like they did when he fell asleep on the couch watching television.

"Honey, are you okay?"

And then, an unfamiliar voice. "Ma'am, this man has been in an accident. Are you his wife?"

"Yes, but—"

"Ma'am, I'm with EMS. Your husband seems to be all right. He's talking to us. If you'd like to meet us at the hospital . . . ."

I took a deep breath and gathered my thoughts from remote places. "Oh, yes. I'll leave now. Thank you."

I ended the call and turned to face two sets of round eyes. "Let's go, girls. Change of plans."

A couple of miles from home, my mouth fell open as I spotted his small, white pickup being loaded onto a wrecker's flatbed. It looked bad. Crumpled. In my heart, I reminded myself my husband was safe. "Girls, I just talked to daddy — he's okay — so let's get to the hospital and tell him how much we love him."

Lord, he was two miles from home. Two miles.

After an eternity of insurance and paperwork, I was ushered to the bedside of a man in distress. His brow was furrowed, his head turning from side to side. When he saw me, his face lit in recognition. "Honey, where are the girls? Were they hurt?"

Confused, I took his hand. "The girls are fine. You were on your way home from work."

Not convinced, he continued to plead. "Tell me the girls are okay."

I looked to the medical staff for help. A nurse shrugged and shook her head.

In minutes, I watched the love of my life slip further and further away.

His brain was swelling — logic and memories fading. After he stopped asking about the girls, he told me over and over of his love for me. How thankful he was for our lives together.

Then, even my familiar face faded and his eyes darted wild and unseeing. His voice was lost, alone. He called out to all that was left to him. "Oh Lord . . . "

He was echoing the prayer of my heart.

The next hours were a blur of white coats with their tests, speculations, and consultations. The decision was made to transfer Roy to a larger hospital, an hour away in Raleigh. By this time, he seemed to be sleeping. I refused the word, "unresponsive."

By 10 P.M. we faced a new facility — a maze of halls, rooms, sights, and sounds resembling a small city. Every two hours, hospital rules allowed me fifteen minutes by my husband's side. And each time I walked through the doors of intensive care, the questions swirled. Will he know me? Will there be a flicker of recognition? Will the doctors have any answers? I leaned heavily on Isaiah 26:3: *You will keep in perfect peace those whose minds are steadfast, because they trust in you.*

Time slowed and moved as a sea of thick sludge. As my girls and I paced each inch of the waiting room, worry and sleep deprivation pulled at my thoughts. This wasn't how I envisioned the days before Christmas. The usual swirl of parties, church programs, and shopping trips seemed like a fuzzy, far-off dream.

My over-tired eyes felt dry and gritty as I looked at my watch for the hundredth time — 4 A.M. Our extended family remained scattered around one side of the waiting room in various states of shallow sleep. The girls tried to doze in stiff, wood-framed chairs not designed for comfort. The air seemed stale and my stomach turned from the bits of vending machine food I'd forced down.

Restless and beyond exhaustion, I found a corner to be alone, and surrendered to the flood of emotion I had pushed aside for nearly twelve hours. Myriad doubts and "what ifs" joined forces to attack the protective wall around my heart — a wall that was crumbling from fatigue and worry. *What if he doesn't awaken? What if he wakes but is not himself? What if his brain injury never heals? What if he never fully comes back to us?*

In that moment, the fears, worries, and concerns seemed stronger than my flickering hope, and in the heavy darkness of my heart, I cried out to my Creator. *Lord . . .*

A wave of anxiety swept over me and I couldn't form a coherent prayer. I simply laid bare my inmost self. *Father God, I'm scared. Nothing is changing. It's been hours and he's still not waking up. Help me focus on You.*

As the minutes crept by, I remained still and quiet.

I'd heard people speak of being in the eye of the storm and I'd always thought of those words as cliché. But in that moment, a holy stillness covered me and I was filled with the most hopeful peace.

My sweetheart was still entangled in tubes and monitor wires. My precious girls were still draped over chairs in a hospital waiting room. The unknown still churned around me. But God's Presence lifted me from my circumstances and I *knew* that His love was ever-strong and unbreakable. Everything would be okay. Despite the outcome.

The chains that kept me from forming a prayer seemed to fall away. *Father God, I love You. You are here and Your love surrounds us. However he comes back to us, I will be grateful. I will rest in Your plans. Father, I long for Your will, Your way, Your heart.*

I returned to my family and continued our vigil.

Somewhere around 6:00 A.M., I pushed through my sleepless daze and approached Roy's curtained-off area in intensive care. His face remained still and pale, his breathing shallow.

I stood by his bed and rested in the moment.

And then, as if he had been napping, his incredible blue eyes opened and his gaze collided with mine. I leaned in for the sweetest whisper I'd ever heard. "Hey."

I dissolved into sobs of joy and relief, unable to talk. Roy misread my tears and breathed out in panic, his face twisted in pain. "Tell me the girls are okay."

Squeezing his hand, and struggling to speak through the tears, I finally choked out, "Baby, the girls are *great*."

Oh, the sweet celebration! Oh, the tears and praising God!

More tests needed to be run and his head trauma required more time in the hospital, but he was *back*. God had brought him back to us.

Days later, in the most surreal of moments, our little family stood with other worshippers at our church's Christmas service. Many things were the same — the hymns sung, prayers offered, and the love expressed from family and friends.

But a battle-weary, emotionally-exhausted family experienced a deeper level of gratitude for God's great love and for the gift of His Son because the anchor of hope found in a quiet hospital waiting room was born in the most unlikely of places — a hay-filled manger.

24

For His Glory

Nanette Thorsen-Snipes

Snow dances beneath pregnant clouds,
Spreading a swaddling blanket
Upon the earth —
While footsteps of a Child
Quicken in my heart.

Angels welcome this Child,
Pure as the radiant snow —
Who still displays everlasting love
In each newborn snowflake
Pirouetting for His glory.

25

Paradoxical Peace

Diana C. Derringer

He will proclaim peace to the nations.

Zechariah 9:10 NIV

We read, sing, and dream of peace on earth throughout the year but especially during Christmas. Yet, never in history has our world known earthly peace.

Nations fight nations. Ethnic groups throw slurs, stones, and worse. Families ignore commitments, ridding themselves of one another as easily as they discard old clothes.

Teams replace teamwork with a me-first attitude, regardless of the impact on other players or their fans. Workers undermine bosses and co-workers, destroying reputations in the wake of their climb up the corporate ladder.

Politicians split into *us* versus *them*, creating havoc for the governments and people they were elected to serve. Courtrooms overflow with charges of murder, rape, assault, theft, and a never-ending stream of lawlessness and contempt for the rights of others.

Churches proclaim God's message of love, joy, hope, and peace, yet fight without and within. Such constant blaming, bickering, and breaking down of relationships make the celebration of peace questionable.

Nevertheless, in the Old Testament we read Isaiah and Zechariah's prophesies of peace. In the New Testament Luke details the angels' proclamation of peace at the birth of Jesus. Despite our world's distress, their words remain as relevant today as the night of Jesus' birth.

Everyone who experiences God's salvation knows peace that transcends any circumstance. As Paul tells us in Ephesians 2:14, Jesus is our peace. When we allow His presence to reign in our lives, we enjoy true peace, whether the world around us is peaceful or not.

When we hurt, Jesus' peace eases our pain. When we face death, His peace provides comfort and reassurance. When we endure abuse, He wraps us in His arms of peace. When darkness engulfs us, we walk by the light of His peace. When persecuted for our faith, we can respond with and proclaim His peace. When we fall flat in failure, He picks us up, dusts us off, and tells us to try again — to go in His peace. We celebrate daily the peace made possible through God's all-sufficient gift of grace.

In addition, we look forward to the everlasting peace Jesus will usher in at His return, when all conflict and pain will disappear for those who follow Him.

We cannot know peace on our own. Only when we confess Jesus as Lord will He cover us in His peace. Through Jesus' power, we can pray and live the prayer many attribute to Saint Francis of Assisi:

> Lord, make me an instrument of your peace;
> Where there is hatred, let me sow love;
> where there is injury, pardon;
> where there is doubt, faith;
> where there is despair, hope;
> where there is darkness, light;
> and where there is sadness, joy.

26

Child's Coat, Size 3

Lynn Watson

I've sold everything I own, and I'm going to Rwanda," the lady shared with us at the Christmas party. "I'll be staying with a pastor and his family there. They have four little girls ages two, four, six, and eight. God clearly told me I would take a dress to each of the girls, and some would come from someone I do not know. This person would know nothing of my plans." She held up the gift I had brought. "Do you think maybe these dresses are the ones?"

The question made for a surreal moment.

My story began a few months earlier before I met this woman. I had read about Dorcas in the Bible countless times before, but this time was different. This scripture caught my attention:

> In Joppa there was a disciple named Tabitha (which translated in Greek is called called Dorcas); this woman was abounding with deeds of kindness and charity which she continually did. And it happened at that time that she fell sick and died; and when they had washed her body, they laid it in an upper room. Since Lydda was near Joppa, the disciples, having heard that Peter was there, sent two men to him, imploring him, "Do not delay in coming to us." So Peter arose and went with them. When he arrived, they brought him into the upper room; and all the widows stood beside him, weeping and showing all the tunics and garments that Dorcas used to make while she was with them.
>
> Acts 9:36-39 NASB

Widows and single moms in the seaport town of Joppa may have been low on cash, but they knew the lady who would meet their clothing needs. A disciple of Jesus Christ, Dorcas continuously spread kindness and charity, using her gift of being able to make garments for the needy in her town. She set an example of sharing with the less fortunate. When she became sick and died her friends displayed amazing love for her and cared for her body according to their customs, and they immediately sent for Peter.

By displaying the garments Dorcas had created, the friends showed Peter the kindness of Dorcas' heart. Moved by their tribute, Peter prayed. Dorcas opened her eyes and sat up. Peter helped her stand, called the others into the room, and showed them at Dorcas was alive. The account continues through verse 43. News of that event spread quickly and many believed in Jesus because of Dorcas' story.*

Girls learn skills with a needle and thread while sitting at the feet of their moms and grandmas. I too, learned the skill of sewing, and during this particular reading of the account, God spoke to me as clearly as I have ever heard. "Make two little girl's dresses just like Dorcas did."

"Sizes?" I asked.

"Maybe a two, or a four, or a six," came the response. I settled on sizes two and four.

God provided me a virtual snapshot of the dresses, too. While sewing projects are quite a normal part of my world, when I began this project, my family was convinced I was crazy. We knew no one who could wear the dresses. What a ridiculous effort and waste of time and resources, right? Feeling a bit unsure myself, but knowing I had heard God, I made them anyway.

Along with an invitation from a friend to join her at a women's ministry Christmas party came instructions to bring a Christmas gift for Jesus. The Spirit in me knew the dresses were the gift. The woman traveling to Rwanda also attended as a guest, and that's where we met.

When time came to open the gifts, mine required explanation. I told the story, but only God could bring our lives together in such an amazing way. I'm not certain how I responded to the woman's question, but I know it was in the affirmative. A room full of women experienced God's anointed presence, and those dresses were on their way to bless two little girls across the sea. *

The rest of the story:

While perusing catalogs for a girl's dress pattern that looked like the vision I had been given, God stopped me on a page with a coat pattern. "Make this, too. Size three, blue corduroy with a black velvet collar trimmed in white lace."

"Really, God? I'm unsure why I'm even making these dresses except I'm doing what you asked. And now another specific request? How about I finish the first project, and then you and I will have another conversation about the coat?"

I purchased the pattern and fabric and sewed the dresses.

Our church had acquired several children's names from a prison ministry's angel tree. Each child had a parent in prison. The parent applied to participate in the program. The prisoner's child would receive a Christmas gift "from them" via others in the community prepared to respond in love. Two of us took on the coordination of the effort.

Betsy called all the caregivers of the children to determine a special gift for each one.

When she called me with the list, we knew many in our small congregation would eagerly accept the opportunity to participate. After sharing about twenty requests for fun toys, bicycles, and such, Betsy came to the last name on the list. I heard hesitation in her voice. "I'm not sure anyone will want to take this one."

"Really? What could be so different or difficult?" I asked.

"The grandmother told me the little girl needs a coat, size three."

"She's mine."

Betsy already knew the first part of the story. I shared the rest, and together we marveled at how God works. I'm still not sure why that appeared to be an odd request, except for God working in both of our lives. Had Betsy just listed it as another request without preface, my response may not have had the same impact.

A few days before the big day, Betsy and I delivered the gifts to the caregivers to have under their trees on Christmas morning. We arrived at the grandmother's well-appointed home in a beautiful, stately old neighborhood. She graciously greeted us and thanked us for the gifts, while attempting to hide the pain and embarrassment about our Prison Ministry that prompted our visit. She directed our attention to her living room where a recent portrait of the precious child was displayed.

God again displayed his magnificence!

She was wearing a beautiful lace-trimmed plaid dress in blue, black, and white. The coat would perfectly match her dress.

27
Memories of the Manger

Beverly Hill McKinney

As I unpacked boxes after our recent move I found the box containing our small manger scene. When I opened the box, it seemed memories poured out with each piece. This set had belonged to my parents and was given to me shortly after my marriage. Since they no longer had room for a large tree they had wanted me to have it, knowing I had cherished it as a child.

"I wonder if we should get a new nativity set this Christmas," I said to my husband, Jim. "It's getting pretty beat up. Baby Jesus' foot is missing, a wise man's head is broken and paint scraped off his robe."

He reminded me, "There are lots of memories attached to that one, especially for you."

Memories began flooding in. When I was a child, Christmas celebrations starting with getting out the manger scene in preparation for our cut pine tree.

We spent many hours in the pine forests around our town looking for the perfect tree to put in our large front window, and we always managed to fine one. Then we would carefully unwrap our little manger scene and place it in front of the Christmas tree.

Our family had a tradition that we would each give something special, either handmade or bought to our brothers and sister. My brother, Al, was very creative about wrapping and giving gifts. Every year he would come up with clever gifts that kept each of us guessing.

One Christmas I looked around the tree for my small gift from Al. I could find nothing. As I searched under the tree I realized maybe he had hidden it on a branch. Sure enough, there hung what looked like an ice cream cone wrapped in tinfoil.

I was in junior high at that time and could not imagine what his gift could be. On Christmas morning, as I unwrapped the gift, there sat a tennis ball on an empty ice cream cone. Tucked inside the cone was small stick cologne.

Christmas was a special time in our home. My family attended church regularly and all of us were involved in various Christmas programs either at church or school. We would anxiously study our parts for the plays and Mom patiently listened as we stumbled over each line.

There were many Christmases that I will not easily forget. I remember one year when my folks had very few funds for gifts. We all wondered what we would receive for Christmas. There was always one special present. What would it be this year? I remember that I was happy as I opened my gift and discovered a large coloring book. How I loved to color! My sister, who was the tomboy of the family, got a little collection of cars. We each thought we were blessed.

In the midst of all the merriment and gifts, the folks would remind us that we were celebrating the birth of Christ. We spent time singing Christmas carols and playing them on our instruments.

Our family formed a band with my brothers, Cal on cello, Al on trumpet, my sister Zoe and me on violins, and Mom playing her viola. Dad was our audience and would smile, clap and encourage us to play his favorite carols.

On Christmas morning, as Mom began breakfast, Dad would get out the family Bible and we all gathered to hear him read the Christmas story. Sitting around our tree with our small manger in front, we thought about that special time when our Savior came to earth.

Mom, Dad and my brothers are gone now, but my memories are still vivid of those special Christmas mornings. As I look at my little tattered manger scene, I know it's something I will keep and display. It seems to glow with the memories of the past and will always have a special place as part of my family's Christmas.

28

Opening Doors in the Neighborhood

Kathleen Kohler

Brilliant poinsettias draped over the sides of our shopping cart. Scanning the myriad of color choices, I said to my husband Loren, "How many do we have?"

"Let's see, two, four, six," he counted. "We need two more."

"How about this one for Elroy and Debbie?" I scooped up a vivid pink, labeled Nutcracker. "And Winter Rose Red for Sean and Shirley."

"Okay, let's get out of here." Wasting no time, Loren wheeled the cart straight for the checkout lines. "I think the neighbors will love these," I said, trotting along beside him.

On the drive home I reminisced about our neighborhood's annual Christmas tradition. During the festive season, families who live in our cul-de-sac remember each other by giving special gifts that say, "I'm glad you live across the street from us. I enjoyed our chats over the fence last summer when we were out to mow our lawns."

For nearly twenty years, Craig and Mars had knocked on our door each year and handed us two bottles of sparkling cider with cascades of curly ribbon securing several candy canes. And Shirley, who works fulltime, spends hours in her kitchen baking on her days off so she can share her delicious chocolate-dipped peanut butter balls and butterscotch-coconut squares — a much anticipated treat.

As for Loren and me, we like to include a sprinkling of faith with our gifts. One year we gave neighbors a woodsy-scented pillar candle. Using twine, we affixed red and green gift tags. On one side of the tag we signed our names and on the other we'd written an appropriate verse. "Then Jesus spoke to them again, saying, *"I am the light of the world. He who follows me shall not walk in darkness, but have the light of life"* (John 8:12 NKJV).

My mind skipped ahead to this season's exchange as Loren pulled into our driveway. We hurried into the house, carrying the poinsettias. Seated at the kitchen table, a box of Christmas cards in front of me, I wrote this note to each family:

> We read this story each Christmas to our children when they were growing up. We hope your family enjoys the story as much as ours.
> Your neighbors, Loren and Kathy.

Inside each card I tucked a copy of "The Legend of the Poinsettia."

> The story tells of a young Mexican girl who longed to give something to the Lord. But coming from a poor family she trod empty-handed to church on Christmas Eve. Along the way she stooped beside the path to pick an armful of dried weeds. Upon her arrival she made her way down the aisle past rows of people seated in the already crowded church. Her head bowed, she stepped to the front and laid her precious bouquet beneath a wooden cross. People gasped. Low voices murmured throughout the congregation. "What was she thinking bringing such an unworthy gift?" But God silenced their whispers when a miracle occurred, transforming the weeds into the vivid red flowers we know today as the poinsettia.

I'd always love the century-old folktale that so aptly displays how Christ takes our meager offerings and turns them into beauty beyond our imagination. And I couldn't wait to share the story with our neighbors.

Porch lights glowed across the neighborhood and a gentle snow began to fall one Saturday evening before Christmas. Loren and I walked from house to house, our arms full of cards and poinsettias. Friendly smiles greeted us at each door. "Thank you! Merry Christmas!" echoed behind us as we strolled to the next house.

Since most of us spent the dreary winter months inside, there were few impromptu visits until the following spring. With the arrival of warmer weather, garage doors opened and our neighborhood came to life.

One afternoon Loren and John (name changed) stood out on the sidewalk discussing their current building projects. Part way through their conversation, John grew silent. Staring at the ground, he kicked a rock with the toe of his boot and sent it flying across the pavement. "I've been in jail, you know."

Startled by the abrupt confession, Loren wasn't quite sure how to respond. He whispered a silent prayer. "Lord, please help me know what to say." Always faithful the Lord gave Loren the exact words he needed in the moment. With a smile of compassion Loren said, "John, everyone has a past. The Lord knows I've had plenty of my own failures, and I've worked hard to put them behind me. But Jesus didn't come to condemn us."

Surprised by Loren's response, John relaxed. He mentioned that the poinsettia story we gave them sparked conversations between him and his wife. He confided to Loren how his wife came from a Christian family and grew up in the church. When they first married, her background wasn't an issue, but now with a toddler she felt compelled to return to her faith. However, John had no childhood memories that tied him to God's people and didn't really see the need.

Loren didn't let the opportunity slip by. Instead, he seized the moment to tell John about God's love for him, and shared about our faith and hope in Christ.

John listened. For now, with a young family to raise, John's busy work schedule takes priority in his life. While he and his wife work to come together on their faith, Loren and I pray.

Meanwhile, during the busy holidays, with a flurry of family and church activities, we might be tempted to underestimate the importance of our annual neighborhood exchange. But then, we stop and remember how our token of Christmas cheer stirred the heart of a young family and cleared a path for an unexpected conversation. And so we'll continue opening doors in the neighborhood by showing God's love through our small gifts and sharing the Good News of Jesus.

Significant Though Small

Diana C. Derringer

One little town,
yet a single event
changed the world and its history
through the Son whom God sent.

One ray of light
in a star-studded sky
directed those seeking
God's Promise brought nigh.

One unknown girl
without status or fame
became mother of Messiah
as the angel proclaimed.

One tiny babe
with no bed of his own,
the Good News incarnate,
earth's gift from God's throne.

Any life deemed by others
as meaningless and small
gains significance and purpose
by following God's call.

30

A Christmas Confession

Sylvia Melvin

As December approached, I experienced a premonition that grew stronger each time I entered our church. The annual Christmas program was without a leader this year. The tiny voice that dwells within the deepest part of my consciousness whispered that I would probably hold that honor before the week was out.

I suppose it was inevitable. I had been teaching a junior class, was a relative newcomer to the congregation, and others had not eagerly rushed forward to offer their services. For some unexplained reason, it is extremely difficult for me, when in a divine sanctuary, to refuse to help a group of children who are supposed to be looking forward to the singing, recitations, and playacting.

Any hesitation on my part was met with the usual assurance: "We know you will do a marvelous job, and there will be plenty of help."

The following day found me at the city library, which apparently decided decades ago never to stock their shelves with Sunday School Christmas programs.

Strike one.

Telling myself that surely the church library would have ample material, I confidently inquired. The best they could offer was a catalog of pamphlets that had to be ordered four to six weeks in advance. That was little consolation since the program was scheduled to be held in three weeks.

Strike two.

At the point of tears, I wandered aimlessly down the street until I peeked through the window of a tiny bookstore. My gaze rested upon a ceramic crèche, beautifully displayed among religious books and pictures. Silently praying that I would not strike out, I entered and pled my case. I thought there was a suspiciously angelic look about the lady who helped me out of my dilemma. I would gladly have given her my life savings for the material she showed me.

The program would go on!

My enthusiasm actually peaked one evening as I sat down and read the kindergarten recitations of welcome, the choral readings depicting the nine letters in the word Christmas, and the meaningful message of the Nativity play. Reality soon brought me out of my euphoria though, as I learned that assigning each child to a part on paper is an entirely different story than the actual process. The first child offered no hesitation in telling me he would not take part. The second echoed the same sentiment. Crushed, I finally had to resort to a lecture on Christmas spirit and individual responsibility.

The multitude of promised-help turned out to be the janitor, who offered to set up chairs the night of the performance, and a reluctant teenager under direct orders from his parents to pull the curtain at the appropriate times.

Organizing a time for the practice sessions was like trying to fit eight days into seven. The competition among the church and school programs and the usual holiday festivities was stiff indeed. The night fog moved in, and forced a cancellation of a badly needed practice, was a test of my endurance.

Down to two days before the concert, voices that normally could be heard the distance of a football field merely whispered on the stage. During the singing, the only one who could be heard above the piano was me. I really hadn't planned on singing a solo.

One particular child kept crossing his legs and shuffling from side to side until I reminded him that a dance routine was not in order for one of the wise men. As it turned out, nature was calling him.

When at last the primary class stood perfectly and could actually be heard to the back of the room, the city of Bethlehem, painted on mural paper, tumbled down around them. I learned an invaluable lesson that evening: put your trust in the Lord — not in masking tape.

Finally, the day of reckoning came. Butterflies the size of eagles danced in the pit of my stomach. I had a haunting feeling that the reputation of the entire denomination rested on this presentation.

Slowly, the curtain parted. No turning back.

Yes, there were the usual forgotten lines and cases of stage fright, but my confidence returned as eight young faces captivated the audience with their singing about the birth of Jesus. The hurdles and frustrations experienced earlier were no longer so important. It all fell into proper perspective. No stars were born on the stage that night, just memories of angelic voices to last a lifetime.

31

Grandma's Enchanted Christmas Gifts

Ethel Lytton

Our first glimpse of Grandma's farmhouse came when we pulled through the first pasture gate. We all stretched our necks to see who had arrived before us; it was difficult to be certain since the mile-long driveway wove through two pastures. But we knew Grandma would be glancing toward the driveway to see who was arriving.

After opening and closing the second gate, we were beyond excited. I think daddy was glad when he parked the car and his three chattering children piled out. Relatives came out of the house, but they allowed Grandma to hug us first. Babbling all the way, we turned toward the aromas floating from the front door. It was wonderful to be with our family. Mama had seven siblings, most of whom were married, which meant I had a gaggle of cousins to play with.

Christmas Dinner was a big affair in our family. We gathered around the long dining table and Grandma asked Daddy to bless the food. When Daddy said Amen, we sat down to eat. Grandma usually had ham, sweet potatoes (from her garden) with brown sugar and butter (which she had churned), mashed potatoes (also from her garden), macaroni and cheese, macaroni salad, potato salad (again, potatoes and onions from her garden), green beans (her garden), green peas (her garden), chow-chow (cabbage from her garden), sweet pickles (the cucumbers from her garden), deviled eggs (from her hens), biscuits, cornbread, sugar cookies and gingerbread men.

She made an array of pies: chocolate pie with meringue topping (egg whites from her hens), coconut pie with meringue topping, blackberry cobbler (from Grandma's berry picking last summer), and apple pie (from her trees) topped with whipped cream (from the whole milk her cows produced).

The all-time favorite dessert of the family, though, was banana pudding made from scratch, cooked on the stove with whole milk, bananas and vanilla wafers added in layers after the pudding had cooled.

The first Christmas Tree Lights I saw were at my Grandma's farm in Virginia in the 1950s. The first known electric Christmas lights in America were created by Edward H. Johnson who worked with Thomas Edison. Johnson had red, white, and blue lights the size of walnuts made for his Christmas tree on Fifth Avenue and displayed on December 22, 1882. Grandma's bubble lights were shades of red and green and were mesmerizing, almost putting me in a trance. I preferred watching them to playing with my cousins. It was a magical time for this farm girl.

Grandma's Christmas tree stood in a corner of the dining room where we could watch the lights as we ate the wonderful food she had created from scratch. It took almost two hours for everyone, about thirty-three people, to eat and another hour to clean the kitchen and try to find a place for leftovers. Then everyone would disperse to their chosen areas: the men to the living room with the fireplace; the women to the living room with the wood stove; and the children outside if it wasn't cold and snowy, or around the Christmas tree with me. Later, the adults circulated to talk with a different group. Grandma's happiness could be heard throughout the farmhouse.

Supper at Grandma's meant eating leftovers from lunch. When we waddled home we were stuffed! And happy!

We had received unconditional love, food prepared by her hands, and the first Christmas lights we had ever seen — all Grandma's unforgettable enchanting Christmas Gifts.

32

Season's Greetings

Lola Di Giulio De Maci

I love greeting cards. Especially Christmas cards.

I have a beautiful crystal, see-through bowl in the shape of a swan that sits on the top shelf of my kitchen cabinet until Christmastime, when it makes its way to the center of the coffee table in the family room. Little by little, the swan's wings turn into the colors of Christmas, as each newly-arrived Christmas card is added to the bowl, painting the wings with the colors of this special season.

The red of Santa's suit.

The green of fir tree branches.

The gold of a baby's halo.

The blue of a Wise Man's robe.

Many mornings I sit in the shadow of the Christmas tree's branches while having my breakfast and read each card that has made the swan more colorful and graceful in its appearance. I read the publisher's verse that is printed on the card and reread the personal notes that are penned from the sender. Each card becomes a kind of prayer book for me. Each word a living prayer. I pray for that friend who thought of me during this holiday season and took time to remember me with a season's greeting. I pray they can feel my love and appreciation for their thoughtfulness.

When the twelve days of Christmas come to a close, the crystal swan makes its way back to its nest in the cabinet, and I place the cards it once held in a holiday gift bag next to my chair, ready for visiting throughout the year.

I love reading Merry Christmas messages under a hot, summer sky.

They rekindle in my heart the sacredness of when the Magi followed a star to find the newborn king so they could worship him . . . a time when the miracle of Christmas was born.

33

The Jesus Tree

Deborah Slate Ginder

Shimmering icicles and a coverlet of snow.

Snuggled deep into a Blue Ridge Mountain valley, our little brown farmhouse looked like a Christmas card. An ancient holly — gnarled but green and fancy with its tiny orbs of red — stood sentinel by the flat stone step to the front porch.

A cardinal flashed like a flame in the ice-covered bushes beside our singing stream. But only the stream could manage a song on that chill December morning.

Fear and depression, cold as the snow and dark as the hemlock shadows, hung like a tattered curtain around my heart. I had thought the move from noisy-city-hurry to sweet-Appalachian-slow would make a difference. But the man, my husband, remained Almost-Always-Angry, and I had becoame Please-Lord-God-Won't-You-Help-Us.

I didn't know its name was abuse. I only knew it hurt, and I felt powerless to stop it.

Valiantly I waved as my visiting Mama, the man, and our firstborn son headed into the frozen forest to look for a Christmas tree. The toddler and I stayed behind. He was too young. The drifts were too deep. And I was too shriveled in soul.

As I paced the wide, pine boards that a hundred years of footsteps had worn down, I prayed out loud with tears. Told God how pathetically craven I was. Repented of my cowardice. Explained how much I had longed to ask the man to bring back two trees. Knew in my heart I ought to ask for two trees. But couldn't find the courage to ask for two trees.

So, Lord-God, please, I'm begging You for two trees. You won't call me vile and loathsome names. And You won't smash and bash the boys or me. So please forgive my failure, and won't You, kindly, somehow send me two trees? You're the One who put them in my heart — one for regular; one for a Jesus tree.

I had read it in *Guideposts*: Decorate a tree with things that speak of Jesus. Make it a tradition. A sign that life won't be forever winter. That a Baby came to make it spring again. That He died and rose to make us live again.

They called it a Jesus tree.

Hours passed before I heard the stomping of boots on the flat stone step. I opened the door, and Mama quickly whispered to act like I was happy with it. The man placed a fine, tall pine tree by the door.

But my eyes were drawn to the miracle moving in our front yard — where a cardinal flashed like fire in the ice-covered bushes, and the singing stream raised its voice in praise.

A five-year-old boy in his little brown corduroy coat. A five-year-old boy wearing his red and yellow and blue toboggan hat bright against the snow. A five-year-old boy, plodding through cold shades of white, was gingerly dragging a tiny green tree close behind him.

His eyes reached up to mine, as mine had reached to His.

"I love it!" I ran to tell my child. "I asked God to send us two trees. Oh, thank you, son, for bringing this one home. This is our Jesus tree."

Mama said he saw the tiny tree first thing. And he loved it. He wanted it. The man declared it far too small, and kept on walking . . . looking . . . walking . . . looking.

But my little boy did not forget. Even when the man chose a fine, tall pine, my little boy remembered his first love.

He found his way back to it, and with a tear freezing hope to his bright pink cheek, he asked to bring it home.

Mama said he could.

We made the decorations, the boys and I — cardboard and crayon-colored cutouts: shepherds' staffs and stars and butterflies. The shining crown on top was foil on cardboard, but it shimmered in the darkness where two little brothers slept. Three points upon that crown: Father, Son, and Holy Ghost.

"You heard me!" my heart cried toward the heavens. "You can hear me. You can see us, in this lonely little hollow in the hills. And You know our names. And You feel our pain. And You're with us. You are Lord Immanuel."

There were no lights on the Jesus tree that year, but the Light Himself held us through the winter.

In the days to come, He called abuse by name. And He took us by the hand and led us to a place where we were safe and warm and loved.

Through the years, I've hung angels and lambs and yellow butterflies on Jesus trees shining with peaceful glory. Each time, I cherish the picture I hold in my heart — of that little boy plodding through cold shades of white in a valley, tenderly dragging a tiny green tree close behind him . . . the answer to this desperate mother's prayer.

And a cardinal flashed like fire through the ice-covered bushes while a singing stream lifted its voice to our Father in praise.

34

A Season of Peace

Susan Dollyhigh

Gathering around the kitchen table at the homeless shelter, we lit the purple Advent candle that symbolizes peace. Peace is sometimes in short supply for those living at the shelter. Peace is sometimes elusive in my life as well.

This small group of women and I talked about the different things we use to fill our soul's desperate need for peace: relaxing music, bubble baths, soothing candles, food, cigarettes, and even turning to the escape found in alcohol and drugs. We talked about addictions that had destroyed all illusions of peace — along with jobs, relationships, and health — for some.

We discussed what happens when the music is turned off, the bath water grows cold, and the candle melts down into a puddle of cold wax. We commiserated about feeling miserable after a food binge and how the desire for one cigarette produces the desire for another. We agreed that when the high is gone and a hangover has taken its place, we again search for peace.

As we talked, we experienced a growing appreciation for the wonderful gift of peace. But how do we find true and lasting peace? How do we hold on to peace when our situations are anything but peaceful?

We turned to the Bible and found the answer in Isaiah's prophecy (Isaiah 9:6), that tells us a child would be given us whose name would be the Prince of Peace. The Gospels in the New Testament tell us about that Child, a Savior who is Christ the Lord. Luke (1:79) tells us about the birth and life of Jesus and quotes John the Baptist who says that He will guide us on the path of peace. In his letter to the Philippians, Paul says this peace passes all understanding (4:7).

We reflected on the times when we had turned to Christ seeking peace and how He had always proven Himself faithful. In that small kitchen, with the flame flickering on the candle of peace, that peace began to flicker in our souls as well.

No, our situations hadn't changed, but our minds and souls had been transformed by the peace of God that transcends understanding.

Glory to God in the highest, for to us a child was born and He is the Prince of Peace.

***

Remember this.
When people choose to withdraw far from a fire,
the fire continues to give warmth, but they grow cold.
When people choose to withdraw far from light,
the light continues to be bright in itself but they are in darkness.
This is also the case when people withdraw from God.

~ Augustine

35
Grief in the Celebrating

Rebecca Carpenter

Christmas trees glowed. Sugar cookies enticed guests to eat. Festive decorations glittered. At the annual Christmas gathering, residents of my community arrived to sing traditional holiday songs. Friends at one table moved chairs so I could join them along with another lady who had come alone.

As I talked with my new friend, we discovered our husbands died of the same disease — idiopathic pulmonary fibrosis. My husband, Alan, had been gone for four years and her husband only a few months.

"You are still going through many firsts, without him," I said.

She nodded. I knew the fresh pain. My good friend, Bill, had died of the same disease that day. I dealt with the additional grief of losing a friend, although glad he no longer suffered. Grief from Alan's death intensified after dealing with Bill's death and hearing of this woman's recent widowhood.

When the piano began playing, I pushed aside thoughts of death and concentrated on singing. Most friends at our table belonged to our neighborhood singing group. We sang, harmonized and enjoyed each song, serious and lighthearted.

But as I looked ahead to the next song, my chest tightened. Would I be able to sing it? That song brought tears every year at the Christmas Eve candlelight service. Memories came of so many years when Christmas wasn't happy.

I sang the first couple of lines easily. Then I struggled to hold in the grief. My throat closed. No words would come. Tears trickled. Maybe no one would notice. I averted my eyes.

From my peripheral vision, I noticed someone stand. A friend moved around the table and embraced me in a hug. Tears flowed. I tried to speak but could hardly get out my words.

"My friend died today," I said.

She held me again. Then she returned to her seat.

My tears continued during the rest of the song. But my heart rejoiced at her spontaneous compassion at just the right moment. Her comforting gesture didn't eliminate my festering grief but added a bit of healing balm.

The recent widow handed me a napkin for my tears. I noticed her tears too and patted her arm.

"Why did they let us be together?" she asked.

We laughed. With the brief spell of grief partially broken, we both enjoyed the rest of the singing.

However, I couldn't focus on words of many songs because they were too painful. "The Happiest Time of the Year" isn't for many people. "I'll Be Home for Christmas" doesn't happen in lots of families. There is no one to kiss under the mistletoe.

I want to focus on Jesus and the real meaning of Christmas. To help others who are also lonely and sad. Grief doesn't take a holiday. Whether years ago or only weeks, it ambushes and tries to steal happiness. However, the true joy and peace of the season won't be extinguished.

36

Dear Deere Angel

Terri Elders

All God's angels come to us disguised.

~ James Russell Lowell

"Let's take it easy this Christmas," my husband suggested, leaning back in his recliner. "I don't feel up to doing much. Not our usual big tree."

Surprised, I cast a wary glance at Ken. Since we'd retired to the Pacific Northwest a few years earlier, we'd always set aside a Saturday to pick out our tree together. Though we lived in the Colville National Forest, where we could buy a permit to cut our own tree, Ken preferred visiting a little town to the south with a lot that sold fresh trees from an adjacent farm.

For several months Ken's energy seemed to dwindle. We figured his recent heart surgery might be to blame. He excused it by saying, "Oh, well. There's nothing wrong with a little inertia."

"A little tree might be fine," I said. "We can hang a few ornaments and string some lights. If you don't want to go out, I'll drive the SUV over to pick one up."

A week remained before Christmas, and though I'd already wrapped gifts, mailed cards and planned our holiday meal, I welcomed a good excuse to get out of the house. For several days we'd been housebound with intermittent snow flurries, thick, gloomy fog and single-digit temperatures. I'd admired snow and ice on Currier and Ives greeting cards, but living with winter's side effects had diminished my enjoyment of the season.

Ken's face lit up. "Would you do that, baby? Don't forget to put the car in four-wheel drive and go slow. It's slippery out there."

I nodded. I'd lived most of my life in warmer climates, so had little experience in driving in the snow. It wasn't snowing right then, and the tree farm was fewer than 20 miles away. I'd drive slowly, alert for any deer that could suddenly leap out at this time of year.

Soon, I arrived at the lot, located a trim little fir, thanked the attendants who secured it in the back of the SUV, and started homeward on the two-lane highway, reminding myself not to switch on the cruise control because of icy conditions. Ken, who had lived for decades in Reno and was far savvier about snowy roads than I was, had warned me about that.

My spirits lifted as I envisioned the coming evening. I'd put on Ken's favorite jazz Christmas CDs, heat up some eggnog, and we'd trim the tree together. Ken would affix an angel atop the tree.

I flipped on the radio and began to hum along with "Angels We Have Heard on High," happier than I'd felt all this dismal season. Then snow began to fall, and just as I turned on the wipers, the SUV skidded sideways. Startled, I yanked my foot off the gas pedal and restrained from hitting the brakes. The car slowed, but continued to drift across the left lane, crossed the bank and slid down an incline into a snow-filled field. Although the SUV wobbled from side to side, it didn't roll but shuddered and came to a halt.

It eventually stopped shaking, but I didn't. I sat trembling, peering through the windshield, trying to figure out what to do next. I figured if I shifted into low, I could drive back up the incline. Unfortunately, the snow had banked so thick near the top that I couldn't get the SUV across it to the highway. It slid backwards again. I turned off the engine.

I had no cell phone, so couldn't call for assistance. I hadn't noticed any nearby farms or businesses. I wore only a thermal jacket and ankle boots, so I was ill-prepared for hikes. In half an hour it would be dark. If I climbed up the slope to the highway I might be able to wave down a passing vehicle. That might be my only option.

I put on my mittens and reached for the door handle. Then I saw something plowing through the snow bank. As it neared I could make out a man in a silver parka steering a John Deere tractor snow plow. He pulled aside me, and I rolled down my window. Normally, I'd be afraid to roll down the window if I were in a stalled vehicle. But I had a warm, safe feeling.

He pulled up his goggles and smiled at me. His eyes twinkled, as he shook his head. "Don't worry, I'll clear a path for your car to get through to the highway," he said. "I was working high up the hill on the other side of the road and saw your SUV skid across. Sometimes this stretch of highway gets a patch of black ice. It's invisible, so there's always a danger. I keep an eye out."

He turned around and took several runs up and down the hillside, tossing snow to each side until he'd cleared a path wide enough for my vehicle to navigate. Then he motioned to me to follow.

When I got to the edge of the road I looked cautiously in each direction so that I wouldn't be pulling out onto oncoming traffic. I'd turned on my headlights and prayed no deer would jump in front of me. I had barely enough visibility to get across and into the northbound lane. I looked for the snow tractor but could see nothing but snow and trees on the hillside. I checked my mileage. I needed to drive seven more miles before getting home.

When I arrived, chilled but safe, I related it all to Ken.

"Let's put the tree up tomorrow night," he said. "Tomorrow morning we'll drive down to where you went off the road. Maybe we can see a mailbox with an address, or a side road leading to where your rescuer lives, so we can thank your guardian angel."

Sunshine spilled in the windows the next day. Seven miles down the road I showed him where I'd slid off into the field, pointing out the slope our SUV had traversed. Ken pulled over.

"That's a good twenty-foot slope you went down." He shook his head. "It's a wonder you didn't roll."

I knew this was the exact spot. On the opposite hillside, however, there were no roads, no farms, no mailboxes, and no paths. Nothing.

"That silver-clad man really had to have been my guardian angel," I finally said. "That's the only explanation." I remembered the warm feeling I'd experienced when he'd appeared.

That night we decorated our tree, and as Ken topped it with our traditional angel, he grinned. "Guardian angels are supposed to be invisible most of the time, kind of like black ice. But now we know the name of yours . . . it's John. John Deere."

I laughed. Ken loved assigning names to everything.

"There's no doubt. But let's spell it d-e-a-r, if you don't mind. Because of him we'll have a merry Christmas."

I've driven down snowy roads several seasons since, with no more skids or slides, and no trespassing deer. I believe I've been protected by my guardian angel, my own Deere Angel. Invisible, sure, but I'm convinced he's always near, keeping an eye out.

37
Our Thankful Time

Dave Maynard

As Christians, we're thankful to God for the things that happen in our lives. But how often do we share those things with others?

One way our family does this is with our Thankful Time. At Thanksgiving or Christmas, we always have a family get-together. After we've had a big dinner and opened all the presents, we put the younger children in another room to do something quiet, like watch an appropriate movie. Then the adults gather in our living room. With the lights down low, we pass around a lighted glass candle. When each person gets it, they share something they're thankful to God for in the last year.

Each person takes about a minute. Many people share some very personal things. We have about twenty adults, so it takes some time, but it's time well spent. For those who don't want to share anything, we have the automatic pass rule. So far, no one has used the pass rule.

Many times, several people get emotional as they share the blessings of what God has done for them in the past year. It's also a time when some express love for our spouses, family and friends. The year I was healed of cancer, one of my daughters-in-love thanked God for that. I was very touched as she teared up when she was sharing it. Several times, our daughters-in-love have used this time to announce their pregnancies. Everyone gets excited when this happens, as it's usually a surprise announcement.

One of our family members-by-marriage shared how blessed she was when everyone so lovingly accepted her into our family. She had come from halfway across the country to be married to one of our family members, so she had left all of her family to move here.

Most of all, we thank God for sending Jesus into this world, to save us from sin and give us eternal life. Thanking God is something the Bible encourages us to do. First Thessalonians 5:18 tells us to *give thanks in all circumstances, for this is God's will for you in Christ Jesus.*

As we pass our lighted candle, it's so encouraging to hear what God has done and is doing in the lives of those closest to us. It's always a wonderful time for us to feel the presence and peace of God.

We've met and shared this way for over thirty years. Now, the teenagers and younger children want to be part of it. In fact, we like it so much that we've started having our thankful time at Thanksgiving. At Christmas, we thank God for what's coming up in the New Year.

38

The Lifesaver of My Hard Candy Christmas

Vicki H. Moss

Christmas was coming in our second grade class. My classmates and I had already drawn names out of a bowl so we could exchange gifts before leaving school for our Christmas break. The amount to be spent on the Christmas gifts was fifty cents. And all of us kids knew what we loved that cost fifty cents: a foldout book of candy Lifesavers that held five rolls in each side of the book.

My strategic plan for the big Christmas party was well thought out. I would buy a book of Lifesavers for the name I drew and hopefully, whoever drew my name would gift me with the same.

So excited, I could hardly wait for the party. To think about having ten whole Lifesaver packs, five nestled in each side of the book, made my mouth water. I could make that candy last for a couple of weeks! Thinking myself fairly generous, I thought I might even give away the butterscotch roll to someone else, since it was Christmas and a time to be generous . . . and I wasn't all that fond of butterscotch anyway.

When it came time to go shopping for my school Christmas gift exchange, I told Mother what I needed. "Everyone will be giving books of Lifesavers, and that's what I need to buy." At the grocery store, Mother needed to pick up a list of necessary items for holiday baking and I watched our shopping buggy fill as she chose a bag of assorted unshelled nuts for Daddy to eat — he had fun using the nutcracker — oranges and tangerines for the fruit basket that would make our house smell like Christmas, a pineapple for the Upside Down Pineapple Cake Mother would make which was only one of the many cakes she always baked, along with cocoa, lemon, and coconut for pies, cloves for scoring the ham, vanilla and eggs for cakes and snow cream — just in case it snowed — red coloring for the Red Velvet Cake, and shelled pecans for the cream cheese icing, with extras for the fruit cake. Then there were a couple of five pound bags of sugar for the cakes, pies, and hot chocolate we had to have on cold nights and of course a plump bag of marshmallows to float in the hot chocolate. And fudge. We couldn't forget the ingredients for the homemade fudge. An extra bag of sugar might be needed for snow cream in case that snow did come....

I reminded Mother to get plenty of popcorn — which she loved more than anyone — for TV watching. But the best purchase of all was the red hard candy, shaped like a ribbon, that would reside for a short time in the ruby-red covered candy dish that graced an end table in the living room.

Not far from the hard ribbon candy, I spotted them on the grocery store shelf. Lifesavers. I added a "book" to the buggy and I was all set. Now, if only whoever drew my name at school was shopping for my same gift as well, my Christmas was pretty much going to be fantastic — that is until Santa Claus came and then it would be a dilly. I'd asked Santa for a doll house and had shared that request with my parents.

But there was one more errand to run. Mother was going to splurge. So we stopped by the Brock Candy Company — which we did every Christmas — to buy Daddy a box of chocolate covered cherries because number one: he loved them and it was Christmas. And number two: they were less expensive if bought there during the Christmas season.

The last day of school couldn't roll around fast enough for all of the excited grammar school children. Christmas Party Day had arrived. We sat four to a large table/desk anticipating receiving our presents. The boy next to me ripped the paper off his package, and there it was — a book of Lifesavers. Full of laughter and anticipation, we were all punch-and-cupcake-giddy. I couldn't wait to get mine. Someone at the table cried out in sheer delight over a similar Lifesaver box, "Yes! This is just what I wanted!"

Then my gift was handed to me. A present from a girl named Louise (name changed), it was obvious the package was too thin to be a box of Lifesavers and my heart sank to my shoes. No longer giddy, I tried holding my disappointment in check, and slowly unwrapped my gift. What I held in my hands could only be a book. I loved books. Right? But a book was even better if it had Lifesavers in it!

My eyes beheld a small dime store book, *The Night Before Christmas*. Santa Claus and his reindeer were on the front cover. Along with the price tag. Ten cents. Dime, indeed. Louise hadn't even spent the amount suggested by the teacher. I knew this story, practically by heart. Babies knew this story. I felt like I had never been so cheated. While almost everyone else was enjoying the sweetness of a Lifesaver, I was enjoying the sourness of disappointment and hurt feelings. Why couldn't someone else have drawn my name?

Only seven years old, I tried to regroup, and muster up some manners. Before leaving school, I thanked Louise for my gift though I doubt the smile on my face was genuine, or even if I wore a smile. Later, I tried my best to sort it all out. Why me Lord? Why couldn't Louise have drawn someone else's name? There was my hurt all laid out before the Lord. And my disappointment. Louise drawing my name was the unluckiest incident ever! And though I hadn't yet turned my life over to the Lord with being "saved" and being immersed in a public baptism, the Lord was speaking to me even then.

What was brought to my mind was that somehow — maybe some of the other children had told me — I knew Louise was living with grandparents who were rearing her and a younger sister and they obviously lived on a limited income. No one knew anything about Louise's parents or where they were. That part was a mystery. Louise and her sister seemed less fortunate, when it came to material things, than some of the rest of us.

None of us were wealthy, but most of us had enough. And I knew in my heart of hearts that by the way Louise and her tiny waif-of-a-sister dressed, they could have used a little more.

My heart began to soften. After all, I reasoned, I could always have one of Daddy's chocolate covered cherries. He didn't mind sharing with me. And Mother would soon have those cakes and pies baked. And how could I forget? I had assorted nuts and oranges and tangerines waiting for me in my living room not far away from the ruby-red covered dish that held ribbon shaped hard candy. Maybe this entire Christmas was going to be a hard candy Christmas. Maybe Santa would pull through. Maybe not. He was sometimes a disappointment too, bringing the wrong toys. Hard candy Christmas or not, there might still be a big snow. There would always be cakes and pies, and even if there was no snow and no sugar involved, being with my cousins was wonderful. Plenty of sugar was to be had for all by kissing the chubby cheeks of the family babies.

During Christmas break, even though I was familiar with *The Night Before Christmas,* I memorized the story, word for word, so I could recite it to my younger kin to make the holidays more fun. And a fun Christmas we had, while celebrating the birth of the Savior.

Years later, when going off to college and trying to weed out some of the things I'd managed to horde through the years, I couldn't let go of that little book so long ago received from Louise during the second grade Christmas party. So I kept it long into adulthood.

Many years later when I ran across *The Night Before Christmas* and thought about that Christmas party incident with the lack of Lifesavers, it dawned on me that the Lord, in His sovereign mercy, allowed my disappointment so I could experience one of the best celebrations of all. He had taught me it was better to give than to receive. I'd learned that though a gift might be small and thin and not as costly as some, it could be one of the most treasured gifts for years to come with lessons to be passed down to future generations. That Christmas, and unknowingly, Louise gave me a gift that would teach me one of the best lessons I'd ever learn. To be humble and to be kind. What an event to celebrate with at least a cake!

When I think about Louise today, I pray she has had a blessed life with many uplifting moments — that she was successful and productive with many children of her own to nourish and love.

The most important lesson from that year: Jesus Christ taught me He was the real Lifesaver — the Lifesaver of my hard candy Christmas, the Lifesaver of eternal life — a lesson I will always thank Him for and treasure in my heart.

> *Remember the words of the Lord Jesus, that He Himself said,*
> *"It is more blessed to give than to receive."*
>
> Acts 20:35 NASB

39

Remembering the Greatest Gift

Diana Leagh Matthews

Christmas is Mama's favorite time of year. Although Daddy has been gone for almost two decades, Mama loves to tell us about their first Christmas together. I think one reason is because it makes her feel closer to him.

On their first Christmas, Mama and Daddy had been dating for only seven months, although they'd know one another in high school. Daddy was three hours away at college and missing his sweetheart. He searched for a way to make their first Christmas special. While home during Christmas break, he surprised Mama with a gift each day during the week leading up to Christmas.

Included in the gifts were a variety of candies, food, flowers, and a purple stuffed dog that Mama named Patches. As Mama tells her stories, I think about Patches that became a staple in our home, resting on their bed during the day. I remember holding him on many occasions.

I love to watch Mama as she tells about the gift Daddy gave her on Christmas Day. He presented her an oblong box bearing a jeweler's logo. Mama was in awe, when she opened the box to reveal a beautiful gold bracelet, with black jaded ovals and her name engraved in the center. The bracelet is one she still wears today, almost fifty years after receiving it.

Even today, her face lights up when she wears the bracelet. She is reminded of the sacrifice and love Daddy put into his presents. He provided gifts which have lasted during their lifetime together. During that time, he provided many kinds of gifts for our family and loving memories that have lasted long past his lifetime.

His gifts and his life reminds me of Jesus, who admonishes each of us to offer gifts which will last a lifetime to others. The greatest gift we can give to others is to the show Jesus' love to all those we encounter. After all, the greatest gift we are offered is our salvation, leading to eternal life with Him.

By grace you have been saved through faith. And this is not your own doing; it is the gift of God. (Ephesian 2:8 ESV)

Remembering Mama's special Christmas and the thoughts about gifts that inspires, I'm reminded to give special gifts to others, the greatest of which is love.

40

Foolish Question

Yvonne Lehman

In February, I was sitting in bed working a crossword puzzle. My Pomeranian, Rigel, reclined at the foot of the bed. Christmas music was playing, as it does all year long because he likes it, or else because I don't bother to change the selection on my old phone's Pandora. The music doesn't matter to me so much since it's the time of night I work a crossword puzzle and read.

However, my concentration was broken when a particular male voice began singing a carol. I stared at the phone, enraptured by the singing. My thoughts were, *how can anyone sing like that? Where does such a sound come from?*

I shook my head at the foolish question, a rhetorical question, and cast a knowing glance upward, acknowledging that I know the answer.

Then I looked at the next crossword clue. It asked for a four-letter response to, " prayer ending."

And God answered, "Amen."

Every good and perfect gift is from above . . .

James 1:17 NIV

41
But What If It's Dirt?

Jeri McBryde

"Why do we have presents at Christmas?" my young granddaughter asked.

"To celebrate Jesus' birthday," I explained. "Christmas is a time for giving and receiving. We give each other gifts in his honor."

I waited for her next question. Beth always had a next question.

"What about a cake? Why don't we have a birthday cake for Jesus? One with candles?"

"Some people do make birthday cakes for Jesus as a tradition. Families have different traditions."

Beth grabbed a Hersey Kiss from the crystal sled candy dish. "What's a tradition?" she asked, as she unwrapped the red foil, then popped the chocolate into her mouth.

"That's a tradition," I said, pointing to the dish. "We always fill the sled with Hersey Kisses at Christmastime. It's something we do during the holiday but never at any other time."

Beth looked around and her gaze stopped at the mantle. "Like Joseph, Mary, and baby Jesus in the manger over the fireplace?"

"Right." I smiled at her quick understanding and returned to my task of gift wrapping.

"What about Aunt Grace's yucky dessert?" She wrinkled her nose. "Is that a tradition?"

"Yes, but you don't want to hurt her feelings, so always take a bite and say thank you."

"When I grow up, I won't make my kids eat yucky stuff." She shook her head. "Even if it's a tradition." She wiped the chocolate off her hands onto the sides of her jeans. "Can I help?"

"Sure." I handed her the box of ribbons and bows. "What color ribbon should we put on Grandpa's gift?"

Beth dug through the box and pulled out a wrinkled neon pink bow. "Here, I like this one." She taped the bright bow on the wrapped package.

"He might like gold," I suggested. "It would look nice against the dark green paper."

"No. I like pink." She added another lopsided bow and stood back to admire her handiwork.

"It's about what Grandpa would like," I said.

She nodded. "I picked them out myself," she said proudly.

"I know." I added the wrapped socks to the gifts under the twinkling tree. "And I'm sure he will love the pink bows."

"And Grandpa will say thank you."

"That's right." I nodded. "We always say thank you when someone gives us something. That's good manners."

"And please." She added. "Please and thank you, two magic words that open any door." Beth sang as she danced around the room. A length of pink ribbon and silver tinsel trailed behind her. "We learned that song in school." Then she yelled and came to a sudden stop. "Oh, Gram."

I rushed to her side. "What's wrong?"

"Something awful just came into my head."

"Goodness, Beth, I thought you were hurt." I untangled the ribbon from her feet.

Her eyes teared. "What if someone gives me something I don't like? What if I already have one? What if it's awful?"

I hugged her close. "You just say thank you and when you are alone with Mama, she can put it away. You don't want to hurt people's feelings."

She nodded, then grinned as she challenged me. "But what if it's a rock or even dirt?"

"Then you say thank you for the dirt. It's the best dirt I've ever been given. Then take it home and pour it into the flower bed."

We laughed together and Beth began dancing around the room again. "Thank you for the dirt. It's the best dirt ever," she sang over and over.

On Christmas morning, the family gathered around the tree. Oooh's and ah's, along with thank you's, filled the room among the mounds of paper, ribbon, and boxes.

As the youngest, it was Beth's role to play Santa's elf. That was one of our family traditions. Grandpa, the oldest, would read out the name on the gift and Santa's elf would hand it to the one whose name was called.

Beth was delighted when Grandpa loved the pink bows and the socks. "Now the last present, Beth. It's for you from Gram." He placed the gift in her outstretched hands.

"She tore into the shiny pink wrapping paper and stared in silence. Her eyes widened and her mouth opened. Finally she said, "Look, Gram. These are little bags of dirt. And little flower pots," she whispered in astonishment. "And seeds." She held up a packet. "Look, flowers with faces. White, blue, purple, yellow and red! Aren't they beautiful?"

"They're called pansies. And yes, they are beautiful."

Beth gave me a hug. "Thank you, Gram. Thank you for the dirt."

I pray that is a lesson Beth will remember. What we often see as undesirable dirt may be what God knows will turn out to be one of our life's most beautiful flower garden of blessing.

> Every flower must grow through dirt.
>
> ~ Anonymous

42
The First Christmas Gift

By Norma C. Mezoe

The wrapping was strips of cloth,
the tinsel, bits of hay,
Jesus, the precious Gift of God,
in a humble manger lay.

No colored lights on a green pine tree
shone upon His face....
But in the sky a bright star gleamed
and pointed to His grace.

43
Return of the King

Bob Blundell

I had always imagined a dark barren valley, painted in murky shades of sand and grey, surrounded by harsh mountains with jagged peaks reaching into the sky like tentacles from an ancient sea monster. To the east, obscured by the muted glare of the sun, a mass of armies from many nations would be assembled. Their sheer numbers surpassed any military force that the world had ever seen or imagined. And embodied within the hearts of each, was all that was evil in the world.

On the western edge of the valley, the forces of good were waiting in anticipation, knowing that the battle that had been prophesized years ago, was imminent. Clouds moved swiftly across a sky turned pewter grey, and flashes of lightning split the horizon as if God had commanded that the confrontation begin.

The wind began to swirl around me, carrying an acidic odor of fear and desperation. The earth beneath my feet trembled from the vibration of the machines of war as they inched their way into position. The end, that had been written about, 2,000 years before, was drawing near.

Today, however, I gazed down on that same historic valley. What I see before me is a rich, lush vista with long lines of verdant-green hedgerows stretching to the horizon. The azure sky is pure and cloudless, allowing unfiltered light to warm my face, and a morning dew glistens on the grass like tiny jewels. In the distance, snow-capped mountains gently cradle the valley between their peaks. It was a scene of pure beauty and perfection painted by our Maker.

A sign next to me bore four words: THE VALLEY OF ARMAGEDDON. The dour connotations of Armageddon seemed a contradiction to the visual splendor of the land before me.

I first heard of Armageddon forty years ago when I was a sophomore in college. My life then was a secular existence with no understanding of who God was, or the role He played in my life. Late one evening, several friends and I gathered together and began to discuss *The Late Great Planet Earth*, a book we had read. In that best-selling book from the 1970s, the author vividly described the end of days, the rise of the anti-Christ, and the incredible suffering that would someday exist in a world immersed in turmoil.

I lay awake in my dorm room early that morning, unable to sleep even as sunlight crept through the window shades. As I stared at the ceiling, I felt a vise-like coldness creep into my heart. It was fear.

At that point in my journey I didn't have a relationship with God, and I was certain that I was unworthy of being saved when Jesus returned. Catastrophic images of a world spinning out of control swirled through my mind until I finally succumbed to sleep. That was long ago, before I learned of God's infinite love and mercy.

Now, as I stood above this beautiful valley in northern Israel, I found it difficult to fathom that this idyllic landscape could be the site where good and evil would clash in a final battle, and the glory of God would ultimately prevail.

I closed my eyes and tried to imagine the visions that flashed through Saint John's mind as God gave him a glimpse of His plans for the world. To see the path that the Lord had predestined for us, would have been more than the human mind could possibly understand. Yet through His power, John wrote of it and gave us the book of *Revelation*.

In my favorite passage from his writing, John uses beautiful imagery to describe a vision of the blessed mother of God. He describes her as a woman clothed with the sun, with the moon under her feet, and a crown with twelve stars on her head. I imagine golden rays of sunlight dancing and swirling around her like a brilliant flaxen cloak. And I see incredible beauty and grace in her eyes. There would be a shining crown on her head with twelve precious jewels embedded in it, and she would be bearing the One that would save us all.

Later, John wrote of the ensuing battle between good and evil at Armageddon. The heavens would suddenly open-up, and rider on a horse with a white coat and mane as pure as snow would descend on the earth in a blinding flash of light, with the armies of heaven following him. Their numbers and the power they wielded would be more than the earth had ever seen. They would destroy the evil one, and the world that we know would no longer exist.

I sometimes reflect on that night decades ago as I lay in my dorm room paralyzed with fear, contemplating what the end might mean to an unworthy sinner like me. I wish I had understood that God is the essence of love and forgiveness, as spoken of in the powerful story of the Prodigal Son in the book of *Matthew*. But what's truly important is that I understand and believe it now.

For centuries, theologians have sought after, and philosophized on the true meaning of the visions Saint John wrote of in *Revelation*. Were they allegorical images of the future? Or were they intended to literally illustrate the world's destiny? I used to dwell on these questions, wondering what lay ahead for the world. But I now know, they will be answered in their own time.

As I stood above the valley, to the south of me, lay the blessed setting where our Lord entered this world. As an infant, he was wrapped in swaddling cloth, and cloaked in a veil of humility and grace. From a candle that flickered in the darkness, shadows danced on the walls of the cave. And suddenly a tiny baby's cry pierced the silence of the night. A Savior was born! A King who would conquer the world.

Glory to God in the highest, and on earth, peace to those on whom his favor rests.

As I opened my eyes and absorbed the beauty of what God has created, I saw how fitting it is that the final conflict take place in this land of abundance and life. For it is here where Jesus will return and bring permanent light and joy to all the world. I knelt and felt the red dirt at my feet. I grasped it in my palm, sensing its warmth. I squinted into the amber glare of the sun remembering the verse in chapter 21 of *Revelation*: *He will wipe every tear from their eyes, and there shall be no more death or mourning, wailing or pain, for the old order has passed away* (Author's Paraphrase).

That gives me comfort and solace as I look forward to Jesus' return.

44
Timing the Lights

Kristy Horine

I just couldn't seem to get into Christmas. I dreaded the Christmas decoration box in the attic. I resisted moving my living room furniture to make Christmas fit. I shivered at the thought of checking that many tiny bulbs to see which one was the burned-out culprit. And who was going to dust all these snowmen and red-hat-wearing bears? Add to all this my general discomfort about commercialism, battery sucking electronics, noise, mess and the post-gift haze that hovered in the air while I was left to clean up the Christmas dinner that I almost burned — again.

I think God knew how much trouble my heart would have with Christmas. I believe that's why he gave me Emily.

Emily is my number three child. She loves Christmas. Each year, after she removes her Halloween make-up, she hunts down the Christmas decorations box. And every year, no matter how I try to hide it, she always succeeds in finding the box.

I was the leader of reluctant elves. Resentment poured into my heart at Christmas's intrusion on my carefully constructed life. What had happened to Christmas? What had happened to me?

For years, hope had eluded me. I had given thirteen years of life to an alcoholic husband. Thirteen years full of broken promises and crushed dreams. When I realized the very real physical danger of our situation, and the fact that there was no longer any use in hoping for a miracle of change to occur, we escaped. Suddenly, I was a struggling single mom to three children. Everything took a back seat to survival.

Ultimately, I closed off any extra space for hope because it was easier than being disappointed.

No room for hope meant no room for Christmas.

And then, when I didn't feel like Christmas — or any season at all — my youngest child was there, dragging out the dreaded box. I guess she believed that a little hope and a string of lights would go a long way.

Somehow, for five years after we left their father, she pulled it off. She conspired with my mother to raise trees and decorations and lights in almost every room of our tiny 800 square foot rental home. I relented with the space for decorations, but not the space in my heart.

Slowly, I healed. Very slowly, I trusted again. After years of shutting out hope and anything remotely connected to happily ever after, I remarried.

Approaching our first Christmas, I again had those feelings of reluctance and resentment and remembrance of lost hope. The holidays have a way of bringing memories surging back. They also have a way of letting us see ourselves more clearly, in a raw sort of light. I had healed some, yes. I was happier, yes. I had gotten married again, yes. But I moved through my moments with such guarded optimism that I still didn't dare experience anything to the utmost. Our marriage was practical, sober, safe. I kept my distance from hope. After all, it had let me down before. No use getting all emotionally tangled up with lights and tinsel.

Not so for my new husband. I had married a man who carried with him a pocketful of hope. Eric and Emily hunted every possible Christmas decoration we had. Anyone visiting our house would have assumed the season had exploded in every room of our old farmhouse.

Not long after the last decoration was hung and Emily headed to bed, Eric stayed up to fiddle with the lights. He had bought a timer system just for our Christmas tree.

"I set it to turn off at 7:15 in the mornings," he said, "so the kids can look back and see the tree before they get on the bus. And it will turn on again as soon as it begins to get dark."

For a moment, past fears and hurts and lies melted away. Those words my precious husband spoke were a glimmer of hope for all the Christmases yet to come.

He asked, "Do you think the kids will like it?"

I nodded because I couldn't manage to speak around the lump in my throat. This man who had no biological ties to my children, considered my kids at Christmas. I had longed to trust him more, longed to believe our marriage was more than a practical arrangement. Despite my longings, I couldn't scale all those piles of fear in my heart. Yet, in this one small act, this new man had done for my children more than what their biological father had done for them most of their lives. He had timed the lights to be a blessing for my children. He had timed the lights for them to see. *Just like God had timed the light of Jesus' arrival for all the world to see.*

Suddenly, a simple timer shed light on so much more than our living room. For a moment, I was allowed the grace to think that I had the faith and strength to believe. It wasn't a matter of making Christmas fit. It was a matter of allowing Christmas to flood me with light and hope. Next year, I will likely not be the first person to get the Christmas decorations box out of storage. But for the first time in a very long time, Christmas will be an enormous, light-filled, hopeful thought.

45

Which Figure Are You?

Linda Gilden

"Let's go to Bethlehem and see this thing that has happened which the Lord has told us about."
~Luke 2:15 NIV

"Mom, come here," ten-year-old Mae yelled. "Doug did it again."

I headed back up the stairs to see what was going on. My three children were gathered around the manger scene on top of the piano.

"Look," Amy said pointing to Baby Jesus, "he can't even see out."

"Yeah, and the donkey is way back here. Tell Doug to stop moving all the people around."

Five-year-old Doug was standing in front of the stable looking very pleased with his work.

"Mom, they're singing. See, Jesus likes to hear all the people sing."

"What are they singing?" I asked.

"Oh, Mom," the girls said in unison, rolling their eyes.

"Just a minute, girls, let Doug tell us."

"They're singing 'Oh, How I Love Jesus.'" Doug smiled.

This was not the first time our manger scene had been rearranged. All three of our children had spent time "arranging" the people. Today, they happened to be singing. Sometimes they lined up to give Jesus their gifts. Other times they were far away, just beginning their journeys.

"Doug, why don't we move the people back a little? Let's all help."

I picked up the camel and the camel driver. "See this fellow," I began, "His name is Obadiah. He's had this camel for only a year. That's not long. Usually people keep their camels for many years. This is the camel's first long journey.

"You see how loaded his back pack is? He is bringing gifts to Jesus too. He also carries supplies for Obadiah. When Obadiah gets tired, he has to camp and rest."

Amy picked up the boy carrying his bagpipes. "What about this man? What's his name?"

"That's Thaddeus," I said. "He's bringing a gift to Jesus too. Can you guess what his gift is?"

"Bagpipes?" offered Mae.

"Something in his bag?"

"Thaddeus is bringing the gift of music," I said. "He has practiced and practiced so he can play a song for Baby Jesus and Mary and Joseph."

Doug picked up a man holding a sheep in his arms. "Is this man going to give Jesus a sheep?"

"Yes, he probably is," I said. "In those days, a sheep was a very fine gift. It meant the family could have wool for clothes and food. Sheep also were sacrificed to God. They were very important animals."

We continued returning the figures to their positions.

My mother had started this tradition in our family when we were children. Mama shared stories about the baby Jesus. She told us about each figure and why they looked as they did. The people came alive as the stories unfolded of the hardships they had endured to make their way to the manger. If one person was not smiling, they too had a reason for their lack of joy. Each piece of Mama's manger scene was housed in its original box marked with a detailed description.

My own manger scene is a collection Mama began for me almost forty years ago. Mama gave me the stable and the Holy Family for my birthday and the rest of the pieces were purchased individually. If you pick up the figures and look on the bottom, Mama recorded the date I received that figure which tells me if it was a gift for Christmas, birthday, or some other occasion.

My figures, like Mama's, often find themselves standing in a different spot each year.

Mae picked up another figure. "This lady has a basket full of eggs. Wouldn't it be hard for her to carry them all that way?"

"Yes, it probably was hard not to break any eggs. But this lady raises chickens. If she has extra eggs, sometimes she trades the eggs for other things she needs."

"What kind of things?"

"If she doesn't have a cow, she may trade eggs for milk. Or she could trade it for flour and other staples. These eggs are all she has to bring to Jesus."

"That's cool," said Doug. "Maybe I could trade some of my stuff for things."

My favorite figure was the one that lived in the box marked "man with headache." He carries a small lunch basket. Clutching his hat, he holds his right hand to his stomach. He holds his head with his left hand.

"See this man," I said picking up my favorite manger man, "he has a headache."

"Why?"

"Well, I don't know for sure. But he worked very hard in the few days before his journey. His wife and three small children are left behind. Along the way, the man hasn't slept very well. This is his first long journey away from his family and he misses them. His children are very young so "man with headache" had to find a friend to oversee his flock while he is gone. Despite the difficulties of the trip (which gave him a headache), the anticipation of seeing Jesus makes it all worthwhile.

We don't really know how many "figures" traveled to the manger. We know that communication and distance kept many visitors from getting there until Jesus had grown a bit. But we know that many rejoiced at Jesus' birth and wanted to meet God's only Son as soon as possible.

Today, I can identify with some of those figures. Sometimes my arms are full, like the lady with the basket of eggs. Sometimes I am pulling a heavy load like the camel driver. Sometimes my efforts to get to the Savior are sidetracked like the young boy chasing the sheep. And, sometimes I have a headache. But each day, if I could pick which figure to "be," it would be the young man kneeling in front of the manger. I would *take off my hat*, bow my head, and kneel before Him, eager for just a glimpse of His glory.

   Won't you join me there?

46
Treasured Keepsakes

Ann Brubaker Greenleaf Wirtz

Christmas and nostalgia are ever entwined.
As the decorations for table
and tree are unpacked,
memories tumble out.

The who, where, when, and how
each item came to be,
that treasured keepsake
I long each year to see.

There's the Santa face my mother handmade,
still sequinned with sparkle
though a half-century old
her love for me is the story that's told.

And placed about are the candles and plates,
the ribbon and holly,
the wreath upon the door . . .
it's Christmas galore!

And always the books are handled with care,
their stories old and reaching back
to a time I contemplate with awe,
their simple message a timeless draw.

> The nativity set completes the décor
> Mary and Joseph and Baby Jesus, so tender,
> Lovingly arranged in a lowly stall
> they tell the reason for it all.

Let us pray:

Dear Heavenly Father,

Thank you for the wonder and glory of Christmas. This season livens our senses and warms our hearts as we see the treasured beauty that speaks to this holiday alone, as we hear the melodies that uplift with holy thought, and as we share the bounty of Your love with others. We ask Your mercy and blessing to bring comfort where loss is fresh, where challenge is great, where need is evident. In a world that is desperate for You, may we be Your instruments of compassion and love.

In the wonder and glory of the name of Jesus, I pray.

Amen.

About the Authors

Shirley Smith Alday is a recent widow who chose to blog about her grief. Her blog, *A Time to Grieve / Diary of a Widow* can be found at www.shirleyalday.wrodpress.com. Several of her stories have appeared in the local newspaper, *The Miller County Liberal*. Her hobbies include genealogy research, sewing for her granddaughters, and archiving family stories, pictures and memories. Shirley is proudly serving as the full time caregiver of her aging parents. She is the mother of two wonderful sons, mother-in-law to their smart and beautiful wives, and MeMommy to the two sweetest little girls and the number one baby boy in the whole world. She currently resides in south Georgia but visits in Pennsylvania every chance she gets.

Max Elliot Anderson grew up being a struggling reader. After surveying the book market as an adult, he sensed the need for action-adventures and mysteries for readers ages 8–13, that would have interested him when he was a child. Using his extensive experience in the production of dramatic motion pictures, videos, and television commercials, Max brings that same visual excitement and heart-pounding action to the stories he writes. Young readers have reported that reading one of his books is like actually being in an exciting movie. Middle grade adventures/mysteries https://middlegradeadventureandmystery.blogspot.com; *The Sense of Humor* http://yourhumorsense.blogspot.com

Candy Arrington is a writer, speaker, and freelance editor. She often writes on tough topics with a focus on moving beyond difficult life circumstances. Candy has written hundreds of articles, stories, and devotionals published by numerous outlets including: *Focus on the Family, CBN.com, Arisedaily.com, Inspiration.org, Healthgrades.com, Care.com, NextAvenue.org, CountryLiving.com sand Writer's Digest*. Candy's books include *When Your Aging Parent Needs Care* and *AFTERSHOCK: Help, Hope, and Healing in the Wake of Suicide*. She is a member of AWSA (Advanced Writers and Speakers Association), CAN (Christian Authors Network), and ASJA (American Society of Journalists and Authors). Read Candy's blog, *Forward Motion*, at https://candyarrington.com/blog/

Bob Blundell is a freelance writer living in the Houston area. He has had previous work published in magazines such as *Liguorian*, *The Living Pulpit*, *The Bible Advocate*, *Testimony*, and *The Avalon Literary Review*.

Lisa Braxton is an essayist, short story writer, and novelist. Her debut novel, *The Talking Drum*, is forthcoming in spring 2020. She is a fellow of the Kimbilio Fiction Writers Program and a book reviewer for *2040 Review*. Her stories and essays have appeared in *Vermont Literary Review*, *Black Lives Have Always Mattered*, *Chicken Soup for the Soul* and *The Book of Hope*. She received Honorable Mention in *Writer's Digest* magazine's 84th and 86th annual writing contests in the inspirational essay category. She earned her Bachelor of Arts degree in Mass Media from Hampton University, her Master of Science degree in Journalism from Northwestern University, and her Master of Fine Arts degree in creative writing from Southern New Hampshire University. She is a former newspaper and television journalist. Her website: www.lisabraxton.com.

Rebecca Carpenter is a grandmother, widow, retired teacher, writer, and traveler who lives in Central Florida. After her husband and parents passed away within a short time, she compiled several of her devotions into the book *Ambushed by Glory in My Grief*. She has won awards for her writings and several have been published in anthologies and magazines. She has been a member of Word Weavers International for many years. Although her life changed dramatically with the death of her husband and parents, God has provided opportunities for her to serve in several ways in the community and her church. One unplanned ministry is to comfort and encourage those who are grieving.

Elberta Clinton is a retired school teacher and lives in Pennsylvania. She has been married to her college sweetheart for 56 years. They enjoy traveling and spending time with their eight grandchildren, and three daughters and sons-in-law who live near-by. Elberta helps her neighbors as needed, volunteers at church in numerous capacities, is an avid reader and participates in a local book club, tends a flower garden which includes some prized heirloom iris from her native Missouri, is an active DAR member and serves her local chapter as the local American History chair ,and delights in trying out new recipes.

Lola Di Giulio De Maci is a retired teacher whose stories have appeared in numerous editions of *Chicken Soup for the Soul,* the *Los Angeles Times, Reminisce,* children's magazines and books, and columns written for several newspapers. Lola has a Master of Arts in education and English. She writes overlooking the San Bernardino Mountains.

Diana C. Derringer is an award-winning writer and author of *Beyond Bethlehem and Calvary: 12 Dramas for Christmas, Easter, and More!* Hundreds of her articles, devotions, dramas, planning guides, Bible studies, and poems appear in 40-plus publications including *The Upper Room, The Christian Communicator, Clubhouse, Kentucky Monthly, Seek,* and *Missions Mosaic,* plus several anthologies. She also writes radio drama for Christ to the World Ministries. Her adventures as a social worker, adjunct professor, youth Sunday school teacher, and friendship family for international university students supply a constant flow of writing ideas. Visit her at dianaderringer.com. You can find her on Facebook, Twitter, LinkedIn, Instagram, Goodreads, Pinterest, and her Amazon page.

Susan Dollyhigh is a freelance writer and speaker. She is a contributing author to *Spirit and Heart: A Devotional Journey; Faith and Finances; In God We Trust; The Ultimate Christian Living; God Still Meets Needs;* and *I Believe in Heaven.* Susan's articles have appeared in *Connection Magazine, Mustard Seed Ministry, P31 Woman,* the *Divine Moments* series, *The Upper Room* and *The Secret Place.*

Terri Elders, LCSW, a lifelong writer and editor, has contributed to over 130 anthologies. After a quarter-century odyssey, including a decade overseas with the Peace Corps, in 2014 she finally returned to her native California where she lives not far from her beloved Pacific Ocean. Blog: http://atouchoftarragon.blogspot.com/

Ellen Fannon is an award winning author, a practicing veterinarian, former missionary, and church pianist/organist. She originated and wrote the "Pet Peeves" column for the *Northwest Florida Daily News* before taking a two-year assignment with the Southern Baptist International Mission Board. She and her pastor husband have also been foster parents for more than 40 children, and the adoptive parents of two sons. Her first novel, *Other People's Children,* the humorous account of the life of a foster parent, was released November 2018 and is available from Amazon,

Barnes and Noble, and the trunk of her car. She lives in Valparaiso with her husband, son, and assorted pets. She writes a weekly blog on her website: https://www.ellenfannonauthor.com and a biweekly blog for the online *Northwest Florida Daily News*, which has an online monthly readership of 7-10 million: https://www.nwfdailynews.com/.

Carolyn Bennett Fraiser is a writer and graphic designer for Evangelism Explosion International and has published more than 1,500 articles and devotionals in the Christian market. Her work has been included in *Power for Living, The Secret Place, Devozine, Clubhouse,* and *ChristianDevotions. us* as well as in compilations such as *21 Days of Grace* and several *Chicken Soup for the Soul* titles. Carolyn plays the piano for her church and teaches creative writing workshops for teens in her hometown of Brevard, North Carolina. Visit her website at www.carolynbfraiser.com or find her on Facebook or Twitter at @carolynbfraiser.

Linda Gilden is an award-winning writer, speaker, editor, certified writing and speaking coach, and personality consultant. Her passion is helping others discover the joy of writing and learn to use their writing to make a difference. Linda recently released *Articles, Articles, Articles!* and is the author of over 1,000 magazine articles and 19 books including the new *LINKED Quick Guides for Personalities.* Christmas is her favorite holiday when family and friends gather. Linda's favorite activity (other than eating folded potato chips) is floating in a pool with a good book surrounded by splashing grandchildren — a great source of writing material! www.lindagilden.com.

Deborah Slate Ginder is a messenger of God's grace. Her experience as a counselor, missionary, and pastor combines with her personal journey from domestic abuse into a Divinely arranged marriage to produce heart-lifting stories and presentations. Her devotional meditations have been published by *The Upper Room, The Quiet Hour,* and *The Secret Place,* as well as online devotional sites. Debbie lives with her husband Carl in the mountains of Virginia, where they cherish their blended family of five sons and their households.

Phil Gladden writes a weekly column for *The Bourbon County Citizen* on the happenings in everyday life. He lives in the small, laid back town of Paris, Kentucky with his wife, four cats, and two dogs.

Lydia E. Harris has been married to her college sweetheart, Milt, for more than 50 years. She enjoys spending time with her family, which includes two married children and five grandchildren aged 9 to 20. She is the author of *Preparing My Heart for Grandparenting for Grandparents at Any Stage of the Journey*. Her latest book is *In the Kitchen with Grandma: Stirring Up Tasty Memories Together*. With a master's degree in Home Economics, Lydia creates and tests recipes with her grandchildren for *Pockets* magazine and Focus on the Family's *Brio* and *Clubhouse* magazines. She also pens the column "A Cup of Tea with Lydia," which is published across the US and Canada. It's no wonder she'd knows as Grandma Tea.

Melissa Henderson and her husband, Alan, live in coastal South Carolina. Melissa was taught the love of reading and writing at an early age by her parents. She continues to write inspirational stories and enjoys sharing messages on her blog. She has been published in numerous articles and devotionals. Melissa's first children's book *Licky the Lizard* was published in 2018.

Helen L. Hoover and her husband are retired and live in Northwest Arkansas. Sewing, reading, knitting, traveling, pulling weeds from the flower gardens, and helping her husband with home repair occupy her time. Visits with their children, grandchildren and great-grandchildren are treasured. *Word Aflame Publishing, The Secret Place, Word Action Publication, The Quiet Hour, The Lutheran Digest, Light and Life Communications, Chicken Soup for the Soul*, and *Victory in Grace* have published her devotionals and personal articles.

Kristy Horine is an award-winning freelance journalist and writer. In addition to her nonfiction newspaper and magazine publications, her poetry and short fiction have been published in regional journals and anthologies. She was a finalist in the 2018 ACFW First Impressions Short Novel category. Kristy serves on the planning committee and executive board of the Kentucky Christian Writers Conference, volunteers as the ACFW Ohio Valley Zone Director, and is the founder of the 3rd Letter Christian Writers in Lexington, Kentucky. She makes her home with her husband in Paris, Kentucky. Together, they have four children and minister to the Hispanic community through Central Baptist Church.

Sherry Diane Kitts is a member of Word Weavers International and writes non-fiction short stories. Her story, "Free Indeed," received the Loyd A. Boldman Memorial Scholarship to the Florida Christian Writers Conference. Sherry's story, "Big Red," was chosen for an anthology, *Blessings in Disguise*. She writes about navigating life's journey through seasons of labor, love, learning, and laughter.

Alice Klies has written since she could hold a pencil. She is currently president of Northern Arizona Word Weavers. It is through their encouragement Alice began to submit her work for publication. She has had nonfiction and fiction stories published in 20 anthologies. She is an eight-time contributor to *Chicken Soup For the Soul* books and has articles published in *Angels on Earth, AARP* and *Wordsmith Journal*. She has also been featured in the *Women of Distinction* magazine. Alice's novel, *Pebbles in My Way*, a fiction based on her testimony, was released in September 2017. She is a deaconess and Stephens Minister in her church. Alice serves on two non-profit boards: The Professional Women's Group and Sisterhood Connections, LTD. She is a retired teacher who resides with her husband and two Golden Retrievers in beautiful Cottonwood, Arizona. She prays her stories give readers encouragement, laughter and maybe even tears. Her website is aliceklies.com.

Kathleen Kohler writes for Christian and general market magazines such as *Discipleship Journal, Focus on the Family, The Upper Room*, and *School Bus Fleet*, among numerous other publications. Since 2010 she has contributed to 20 anthologies, including 13 *Chicken Soup for the Soul* books, as well as books by Dr. Gary Chapman, and bestselling author, Cecil Murphey. She and her husband live in the Pacific Northwest, and have three children and seven grandchildren. Visit www.kathleenkohler.com to read more of her articles about the ups and downs of life.

Yvonne Lehman is author of 59 novels, and 16 nonfiction books. She founded and directed the Blue Ridge Mountains Christian Writers Conference for 25 years and the Blue Ridge Novel Retreat for 12 years. She is an editor with Lighthouse Publishing of the Carolinas. Yvonne and Cindy Sproles direct Writing Right — A Mentoring Service (WRAMS). Her recent publications include a novella in the collection *The Reluctant Brides* and *Personal Titanic Moments*. Her most popular book is *Hearts that Survive — A Novel of the Titanic*.

Ethel Lytton writes devotions and has been published in christiandevotions.us. She is a member of American Christian Writers (ACW) and Word Weavers International, Madison, Georgia. She is a graduate of Jerry Jenkins Writers Guild Apprentice level and is a former columnist for *Montgomery News Messenger*, Christiansburg, Virginia.

Diana Leagh Matthews is a vocalist, speaker, writer, life coach and genealogist. During the day, she is a certified Activities Director for a busy nursing facility. She is a Christian Communicators graduate and has been published in several *Divine Moments* books. She currently resides in South Carolina. Visit her at www.DianaLeaghMatthews.com and www.alookthrutime.com.

Jeri McBryde loves sharing her life experiences in the *Chicken Soup for the Soul* series with the hope of helping others. Her stories have appeared in 8 *Chicken Soup for the Soul* books: *Family Matters, Devotional Stories for Tough Times, Messages from Heaven, Living with Alzheimer's & Other Dementias, Family Caregivers, The Magic of Mothers and Daughter, Merry Christmas,* and *My Very Good, Very Bad Dog*. Her works also appear in two anthologies *Looking Through the Rearview Mirror* and *Seasons of Life*. Jeri lives in a small southern delta town. Retired, she spends her days reading and working on her dream of publishing a novel.

Dave Maynard earned a Michigan provisional teaching certificate and a Bachelor of Science degree with a major in physics and minors in astronomy, chemistry and mathematics. He has done graduate work in astro-physics, worked as a physics graduate teaching assistant and taught college astronomy. He has worked as a research and development laboratory manager at a plastics company, an automotive engineer, a chemist and a public and private high school teacher in math, physics and chemistry. He is retired from his own advanced materials tooling company. He has taught Christian adult education since the mid 1990s at two churches. He was Director of Adult Education at one church and is now a teacher of Adult Education at his present church. Since becoming a Christ-follower in 1974, he has been an avid student of the Bible, with a special emphasis on apologetics (rationally defending the faith). His website is https://bsssb-llc.com. He and his wife, Patti, have been married 43 years and have three adult sons, three daughters-in-love and nine wonderful grandchildren.

Beverly Hill McKinney has published over 300 inspirational articles in such publications as *Good Old Days, Breakthrough Intercessor, Just Between Us, Woman Alive, P31* and *Plus Magazine*. She has devotions in *Cup of Comfort Devotional Daily Reflections of God's Love and Grace, Open Windows, God Still Meets Needs* and *God Still Leads and Guides*. Her stories have been featured in anthologies such as *Christmas Miracles, Men of Honor,* Guidepost's *Extraordinary Answers to Prayer, Christian Miracles, Precious Precocious Moments, Additional Christmas Moments* and *Loving Moments*. She has also self-published two books: *Through the Parsonage Window* and *Whispers from God: Poems of Inspiration*. She graduated from the Jerry B. Jenkins Christian Writer's Guild and lives in Oregon.

Sylvia Melvin's affection for the written word has roots in her Canadian heritage. She grew up in a small village in Northern Ontario at her family's fishing lodge. Often, books were her companions and she began journal writing as a young adult. Today, although she lives in Florida, she uses those experiences to entertain and educate her readers. Retired as an elementary intervention teacher, she believes that reading and writing go hand in hand. She is also one of the founding members of the Panhandle Writers' Group and has published short stories, biographies, historical fiction, and mystery novels. She likes to take readers to places they've never visited, meet characters who arouse their emotions, and leave them wanting to read more. Sylvia's books are available at Amazon.com.

Andrea Merrell is an associate editor with Christian Devotions Ministries and Lighthouse Publishing of the Carolinas. She is also a professional freelance editor and was a finalist for the 2016 Editor of the Year Award at BRMCWC. She teaches workshops at writers conferences and has been published in numerous anthologies and online venues. Andrea, a graduate of Christian Communicators was a finalist in the 2015 USA Best Book Awards. She is the author of *Murder of a Manuscript, Praying for the Prodigal,* and *Marriage: Make It or Break It*. For more information, visit www.AndreaMerrell.com or www.TheWriteEditing.com.

Norma C. Mezoe has been a published writer for 34 years. Her writing has appeared in books, devotionals, take-home papers and magazines. Norma is a regular contributor to online publications *Ruby* and *Christian Devotions*. She is active in her church in a variety of roles. Norma may be contacted at: normacm@tds.net.

Vicki H. Moss is Contributing Editor for *Southern Writers Magazine*, a former newspaper columnist, author of *How to Write for Kids' Magazines, Writing with Voice, Adrift, Smelling Stinkweed, Rogue Hearts,* and co-author of *nailed it! The Nail Salon Chronicles.* With over 500 articles published internationally, she has written for several magazines and was selected to be a presenter of her fiction and creative nonfiction short stories for three consecutive conferences at the Southern Women Writers Conference held at Rome, Georgia's Berry College. Vicki is a speaker, workshop instructor and is on faculty for writers conferences. Her stories are frequently published in the *Divine Moments* series. For more information visit www.livingwaterfiction.com. Join Vicki on Twitter: vickimoss, Instagram: @vickihmoss Facebook: Vicki Moss, and Pinterest: Vicki Moss.

Lana Newton is a Jesus-loving writer who seeks to point her readers to the truth of God's love and grace in their own lives as she continuously learns these life-changing lessons in her own.

Cheryl A. Paden is a writer of inspirational nonfiction. Her writings have been published in magazines, anthologies, and devotionals. Presently Cheryl is writing a devotional titled *The Gentle Art of Sacred Balance.* Her book *Sacred Balance — A Prayer Journal* is scheduled to be released in 2020. Her experiences include working as a registered nurse, local pastor in the United Methodist Church, and teaching writing at the local community college. Seekingbalancebycheryl.com.

Peggy Park is author of three books, two of which are published in other languages as mission projects for pastors and believers in Pakistan, India, Nepal and Niger, Africa. Peggy has a number of published articles in general and Christian publications. She is a public speaker sharing her spiritual journey as well as various teachings she has worked out along the way.

Lorilyn Roberts is the author of 12 books, including the award-winning *Young Adult Seventh Dimension* series and the memoir *Children of Dreams.* After scuba diving around the world for a few years and earning her college degree while studying abroad, Lorilyn settled into single motherhood, adopting two daughters from very remote regions in Asia. She later earned a Master's in Creative Writing from Perelandra College and is a graduate of the Institute of Children's Literature. Currently, she is President of the Gainesville, Florida Chapter of Word Weavers

International. Lorilyn has rescued many dogs and cats that needed to be loved. When she isn't writing books, she provides broadcast captioning for television. She can be found on the web at LorilynRoberts.com and Twitter @LorilynRoberts.

Bobbie Roper has been a pastor's wife for the past 30 years. She and her husband, Jim, have been married for 47 years, and they have four children and nine grandchildren. She has a Bachelor's Degree in Christian Education, which she received in 2016. Better late than never, right! Bobbie is an inspirational writer who has devotions and stories published in several books. Her passion is to see Christian women grow in their faith, leading to a closer walk with Jesus. She has encouraged women over the years through Bible study, seminars, and as a conference speaker. Her favorite pastime is sitting on her 100-year-old swing marveling at God's wondrous creation as she celebrates new life in Christ.

Leigh Ann Thomas is the author of four books, including *Smack-Dab in the Midlife Zone — Inspiration for Women in the Middle*, and *Ribbons, Lace, and Moments of Grace — Inspiration for the Mother of the Bride*. She is a contributing author in 12 books and compilations and enjoys writing for the parenting websites, *InTheQuiver.com* and *Just18Summers.com*. You can find Leigh Ann on her front porch daydreaming story plots or at LeighAThomas.com. Connect on Twitter at @LThomasWrites.

Nanette Thorsen-Snipes, mother of four and grandmother of eight, has contributed stories to more than 60 compilation books. She loves to spend a weekend in the mountains at a bed-and-breakfast and explore the countryside, especially waterfalls. She has authored one Arch book for children, *Elijah Helps the Widow,* many stories and reprints in Christian magazines, stories and photos for *Georgia Magazine,* and columns for weekly newspapers. A professional editor since 2004, she specializes in children's fiction, nonfiction, and memoirs.

Gina Stinson lived in fear and defeat for many years, but now she is busy reclaiming every day for God's glory. She is a pastor's wife of 26 years and homeschool mom to two teenagers. Between family and ministry, she enjoys dabbling in gardening, crocheting and playing music on her second-hand, baby grand piano. She enjoys writing true stories of God's reclaiming power and is a storyteller for those who have overcome their circumstances and embraced God's goodness. You can find her devotionals in *Journey Magazine for Women*, *Pathways to God* magazine, and several online communities. You can visit her at her website ginastinson.com or through Twitter, Facebook or Instagram.

Lynn Watson has incorporated her love for Jesus and passion for essential oils into the three-volume *Coffee Cottage Inspirational Collection*, where she shares spicy and aromatic essences of Scripture. Her devotions encourage you to diligently cultivate your heart and grow your roots deeply in an intimate relationship with Jesus. Inspired by events in the life of her great grandmother, Lynn is stepping out into the world of historical fiction. She earned a BA in Journalism from Memphis State University, and is also a certified and practicing reflexologist and aromatherapist. She and Steve have been married since 1973 and call Bartlett, Tennessee home. Their lives are blessed with two adult children, their spouses, and five beautiful (of course) grandchildren. Aromas of freshly baked bread often waft from Lynn's kitchen. Jasmine, her tuxedo kitty, runs the house.

Ann Brubaker Greenleaf Wirtz won the Willie Parker Peace History Book Award from the North Carolina Society of Historians for her book *The Henderson County Curb Market*. She is the author of *Sorrow Answered* and *Hand of Mercy*. She is published in *Chicken Soup for the Soul Christmas*, several *Divine Moments* anthologies, and locally in the *Times-News*. She writes a nostalgic remembrance for *The Pulse* every December, featuring her childhood in Webster Groves, Missouri. Ann is the mother of one very dear son and daughter-in-law, and the grandmother of two delightful grandchildren, a girl and a boy. She is married to her beloved Patrick, and they reside in Hendersonville, North Carollina.

The Divine Moments Series Changes Lives, Inspires Readers, and Serves as Wonderful Gift Books for All Occasions

Tell Your Story

We're now accepting articles for:

Christmas Moments – 2020 (anything about Christmas – Santa – Jesus)

Grandma's Cookie Jar (warm, cozy articles reminiscent of the stereotypical grandma feeling)

Broken Moments (light or serious — hearts, lives, promises, bones, mirrors, objects)

Lost Moments (light or serious — way, souls, loved ones, minds, jobs, opportunities, control, objects, arguments)

www.ingramcontent.com/pod-product-compliance
Lightning Source LLC
Chambersburg PA
CBHW070500100426
42743CB00010B/1697